Strategic Review

Strategic Review

The Process of Strategy Formulation in Complex Organisations

ROBERT F. GRATTAN

Gower Applied Business Research
Our programme provides leaders, practitioners, scholars and researchers with thought provoking, cutting edge books that combine conceptual insights, interdisciplinary rigour and practical relevance in key areas of business and management.

Published by
Gower Publishing Limited
Wey Court East
Union Road
Farnham
Surrey, GU9 7PT
England

Ashgate Publishing Company
Suite 420
101 Cherry Street
Burlington,
VT 05401-4405
USA

www.gowerpublishing.com

British Library Cataloguing in Publication Data
Grattan, Robert F., 1931-
  Strategic review : the process of strategy formulation in complex organisations.
  1. Strategic planning. 2. Military planning--Great Britain--Case studies. 3. National security--Great Britain--Decision making--Case studies. 4. Great Britain. Ministry of Defence.
  I. Title
  355'.0335'41-dc22

  ISBN: 978-1-4094-0728-7 (hbk)
  ISBN: 978-1-4094-0729-4 (ebk)

Library of Congress Cataloging-in-Publication Data
Grattan, Robert F., 1931-
  Strategic review : the process of strategy formulation in complex organisations / by Robert F. Grattan.
    p. cm.
  Includes bibliographical references and index.
  ISBN 978-1-4094-0728-7 (hbk) 1. Great Britain--Strategic aspects. 2. Planning--Great Britain. 3. Political planning--Great Britain. 4. Strategic planning--Great Britain. I. Title.
  UA647.G6923 2010
  355'.033541--dc22

2010021051

MIX
Paper from responsible sources
FSC
www.fsc.org
FSC® C018575

Printed and bound in Great Britain by the MPG Books Group, UK

Contents

List of Figures

Preface

I taught strategic management at the Bristol School for some ten years and became particularly interested in how strategy comes to be formed. Although many facets of management are written in text books in a prescriptive fashion, this is not the case with strategy formulation. Students are not given a blueprint to follow, but have to read the descriptions and arguments of eminent scholars, which are usually hedged in with '…it depends'. I cannot claim to have resolved this problem but continue, along with many better brains than mine, to try. I suspect, however, that there is no prescriptive answer in this case because, like chaos theory, small inputs from unexpected sources can have a surprising effect on the final strategic outcome.

I have sought parallels with that other great source of strategy, the military, (with whom I have an association) and have used the theories of strategic management as a lens through which to focus on how grand and strategic management is formed. This was the subject of my doctoral thesis published as Grattan (2002) by Palgrave Macmillan. The Strategic Defence Review is a natural target for such an investigation: hence this book, which seeks to answer the research question, 'How effective was the methodology employed in the Strategic Defence Review of 1997/98?'.

Although we all try to be objective, research is affected by the paradigm of the researcher. Isherwood may have claimed that 'I am a camera', implying neutrality and objectivity, but this will simply not do. The camera records that at which it is pointed and the resulting photograph is a product of the technology and also the skill and intentions of the operator. So it is that this study is affected by my paradigm. I am an Englishman, born in 1931, who grew up in the countryside before and during the Second World, before spending thirty years in the Royal Air Force during the Cold War; serving three tours in the Ministry of Defence. Ten years in the defence industry and twenty in academia have also had a formative effect. This, then, is the 'camera' through which the Strategic Defence Review (SDR) has been viewed, with as much objectivity as could be mustered and with the hope that it has been pointed in the right direction.

Nowadays, much government information is freely available on the Internet and this is a great boon to researchers who can now access these documents in their garrets rather having to make time-consuming and expensive visits to libraries and depositories. These records are invaluable, but one always has to remember that even official documents are not value-free. Some, such as the proceedings of the Select Committee on Defence and Hansard, are verbatim records, but the evidence recorded does not include what the witness could have said, but did not. Records of meetings have gone through the filter of the secretary's (and chairman's) minds, and even the choice of words creates an impression beyond the bare facts. Many of those who actually conducted or participated in the Review are still available and I was particularly fortunate that so many gave generously of their time to talk to me and to give their account of what happened. Their evidence, too, is not value-free and the passage of ten years may have clouded the details somewhat. On the other hand, those directly and closely involved will have had ten years to reflect on their experience and to take a broader view than immediately after the Review was finished. Most of the evidence here then, is qualitative in nature, which will be less than satisfactory to the positivists and empiricists, but that is the nature of strategy formulation research.

After the Introduction, the next two chapters review the theories associated with Strategy and then Strategy Formulation. These form, by their nature, a literature review which seeks to lay down a boilerplate for consideration of what happened in the Review. Most of the theory is taken from strategic management. The nature of defence is considered in Chapter 4. Defence and the military have been with us a long time, which has created a legacy, a precursor, for any consideration of defence policy and Chapter 5 sketches the historical background to the SDR and provides a background for what occurred in 1997/98.

The declared intention of the new government in 1997 was that the defence review would be foreign policy led, and would be as open and all-inclusive as possible, which required a structure capable of handling the diverse inputs that would result. The Secretary of State for Defence and his Department had to orchestrate and evaluate these inputs to produce a practical policy for the military support of Britain's foreign policy. Chapter 5, then, describes the complex structure of committees and groups that was devised to accomplish this difficult task, and goes on to describe how the Review was conducted within this bureaucracy. In the British democracy, Parliament is the body that monitors and discusses the actions of the government, and this task was performed through debates in the two Houses and through the Select Committee on Defence. An account of these proceedings forms Chapter 6.

The views of as many participants as possible were gained through interviews, telephone conversations and the internet, and these inputs provide the fine grain of what otherwise would have been a broad description of bureaucratic structures. Strategy formulation is a human activity, with all that implies in terms of personality, vested interest, subjectivity, objectivity and the whole richness of social interaction. The proceedings of SDR were what they were and it would be pointless to speculate upon what differences might have emerged if 'X' had spoken instead of 'Y'. The SDR process tried to give all the Xs and Ys an opportunity to be heard and it cannot be held to blame if anyone missed the opportunity to affect the outcome. Finally, Chapter 7 is an analysis of the foregoing, leading to a conclusion which seeks to provide an answer to the research question.

Acknowledgements

I acknowledge with great thanks those who took the time to give me their account of SDR from the standpoint of a participant. Invariably they were men and women who hold or held important positions in our public life, and their willingness to talk to an academic researcher was most generous. Sadly, some central actors, notably Air Chief Marshal Sir John Willis, the Vice-Chief of Defence Staff at the time, who oversaw the process of SDR with the Second PUS, have passed away. Sir John was acknowledged as a powerful intellect in defence matters, and I was privileged to count him as a friend. His input to this study is sadly missed. Similarly, Sir Michael Quinlan, a distinguished civil servant, and Air Marshal Lord Garden are no longer with us, and they could have provided cogent comment. Those who did provide an input by interview to this study are listed in the Appendix to this Preface, and I owe them a great debt.

The Ministry of Defence was approached under the Freedom of Information Act for information on the Panel of Experts and they provided a wealth of extracts from their files of the period. Their response exceeded anything I might have hoped for, and I am truly grateful for their generous response.

I have drawn heavily on Jackson and Bramall's excellent account of the British Chiefs of Staff system, which is well-researched, succinct and highly readable. I have referenced much of the use I have made of this book, but their account of the march towards centralised defence policy-making pervades my interpretation, particularly of the inter- and post-war periods. If I have made errors in this process, it is my fault and not theirs.

Air Chief Marshal Sir Joseph Gilbert made some cogent comments on my draft text, and his informed views of defence matters were very valuable.

The University of the West of England continues to support my research activities, and Judith Jordan, Head of the School of Strategy and Operations, in the Bristol Business School, and Professors Nicholas O'Regan and Derek Braddon provided welcomed encouragement and advice. Although many have contributed, the responsibility for any errors, omissions or misrepresentations remain the responsibility of the author, who, nevertheless, hopes that this work nudges our understanding of the strategy formulation process at least some way further forward.

Appendix to the Preface

List of Interviewees

Name	Current Post	Role in SDR
Mr Colin Balmer	Non-executive Director, Qinetiq	Director of Finance, MoD
Mr Jon Day	Ministry of Defence DGSecPol	Director on MoD Policy Staff under Mr Richard Hatfield qv
Admiral Sir Nigel Essenhigh	Chairman, Northrop Grumman UK	Assistant Chief of Defence (Programmes)
General the Lord Guthrie of Craigiebank	House of Lords	Chief of Defence Staff
Mr Richard Hatfield	Department for Transport Director General, International Networks and Environment	Deputy Under-Secretary (Policy)
Air Chief Marshal Sir Richard John	Retired	Chief of Air Staff
Sir Richard Mottram	Retired	Permanent Under-Secretary, Ministry of Defence
Air Vice-Marshal P.J O'Reilly	Retired	Director General, Technical Services President of the Ordnance Board
Lord Robertson of Port Ellen	House of Lords	Secretary of State for Defence
Sir Simon Jenkins	Journalist	Member, Expert Panel
Sir Kevin Tebbit	Chairman, Finnmeccanica	Deputy Under Secretary, Intelligence and Crisis , Foreign and Commonwealth Office

1

Introduction

We are warned against starting any work with an apology but, in studying how conclusions are reached in matters of state, it is perhaps timely to be reminded of the wise words of John F. Kennedy (1963):

> *The essence of the ultimate decision remains impenetrable to the observer*
> *– often indeed, to the decider himself... There will always be the dark*
> *tangled stretches in the decision-making process – mysterious even to*
> *those who may be most intimately involved.*

This study is of the process and conduct of a strategy review and uses the Strategic Defence Review (SDR) 1997–98 as a case study. Although interesting issues such as the structure of the Civil Service, ministerial responsibility, special advisors, economic policies, etc., come to mind, they are outside its scope. The study is concerned with *how* the Review was conducted and *what* resulted is of less interest. The content, however, does affect the process and is considered where necessary.

In studying the special case of the SDR, it is intended that the data and the analysis will contribute to the studies in academia of the difficult subject of how strategy is formulated. The work so far in this field has been largely descriptive and no general theory has yet been propounded. Indeed, it may be that no such theory can be formulated, and Thorngate's impostulate (1976:406) warned:

> *It is impossible for a theory of social behaviour to be simultaneously*
> *general, simple or parsimonious, and accurate.*

The vast volume of data on SDR, given the very large number of people involved, could never be assembled, particularly as some of the notable participants are no longer with us. This study by that measure, is parsimonious. It is as accurate as possible but, by Thorngate's measure, cannot, therefore, be general. Nonetheless, the aim here is to draw conclusions on how the resulting strategy was formulated and to refer back to extant, partial theories of strategy formulation. We proceed by small steps and hope that a pattern will emerge from the totality of strategy process research.

The Context and Setting

The SDR was a product of its time and so it follows that the context and setting for the Review, which are now addressed, are important for its assessment.

The day following the General Election, the outgoing Secretary of State for Defence, Mr Michael Portillo, tidied up his office and prepared to leave the Ministry of Defence (MoD), no longer in office and having lost his seat in Parliament. The news that he was leaving at eleven o'clock that morning quickly spread around the building and the MoD staff gathered in the corridors. As he left, Mr Portillo was loudly applauded: a singular event. The staff then returned to their desks and prepared to work for the new Secretary of State without partiality.

The centrist, New Labour party arose from reforms of the Labour Party whilst in opposition and these involved discarding policies such as Clause 4 (the public ownership of basic industries) and unilateral nuclear disarmament. On defence, New Labour still contained an anti-nuclear group and others were uneasy about the use of military force, although not outright pacifists. One result of this context was that New Labour needed to show to the public and the defence community that it was committed to defence and would deliver a policy designed to meet the nation's needs. Laffin and Alys' (1997) view was that 'Labour's task had been to build a "broad national cross-class appeal"' – an approach that might be seen to be mirrored in the SDR. New Labour sought a national consensus but Tony Blair (the Prime Minister) was quoted in the 'Guardian' (8 April 1997) as saying, 'I accept the need for economic discipline and embrace the role of free enterprise in the economy' – public spending was to be held down. The Opposition needed to be included in this consensus because of the long reach of defence equipment programmes. Mr Richard Hatfield recalled (interview 20th April 2009) the difficulties the lack of such measure of agreement with the Opposition could cause within the MoD. In the view of McInnes (1998:826), however, 'Defence did not figure as a major or even a minor issue in the 1997 general election.'

After the New Labour Party won the 1997 general election and formed a government, it set about fulfilling its manifesto promises, one of which was to conduct a defence review. Their first problem was to devise a process for conducting this review. In opposition, Mr George Robertson had been the Shadow Scottish Secretary but in the government formed by the new Prime Minister, Tony Blair, he was made Defence Secretary, the Foreign Office post going to Mr Robin Cook. Mr Robertson's top team in 1997 were:

John Reid – Armed Forces Minister

Lord Gilbert – Defence Procurement Minister

John Spellar – Under-Secretary of State

Sylvia Heal – Parliamentary Private Secretary

Alasdair McGowan – Special Adviser

Richard Mottram – Permanent Under-Secretary

General Guthrie – Chief of Defence Staff

The defence policy resulting from SDR needed to identify priorities and options which would lead to decisions on force structures and equipment programmes which could be afforded. From the outset, it was decided that the review was to be foreign-policy led, with the hope of cost savings but not controlled by the Treasury, as in many previous reviews. Mr Robin Cook insisted that Britain's foreign policy was to be ethical and that Britain's armed forces would be a force for good in the world (a phrase probably coined by the now Sir Kevin Tebbit, who was then an Under Secretary in the Foreign Office). The whole government aspired to high principles, having made much of the 'sleaze' evident in the previous government.

Another requirement of the Review was that it was to be radical. Sir Michael Quinlan, a previous Permanent Under Secretary in the MoD, wrote to Mr George Robertson on 23rd December 1997 giving propositions for SDR, two of which were:

1.   'The outcome of the SDR needs to be one that has – and is seen
      from the outset as having – a reasonable prospect of substantially
      holding good amid resource constraints and competition through
      at least the life of the present Parliament.

2.   "Little or no change" has little or no chance of being recognised
      as such an outcome by the media, the public, the Treasury and the
      armed forces themselves.'

                              (Enclosure 31 MoD File D/DefPol 16/7/3)

The incoming government appointed a number of 'special advisers' which
affected the relationship of ministers and civil servants. Ponting (1986:243)
wrote disparagingly about the way in which business was conducted in the
'Whitehall village' and had suggested that it was 'still run by a short-sighted
political class and an amateur Civil Service élite, with tools devised in the
nineteenth century'. He was only reflecting the earlier view of Sir Sidney Low
(1904) who had pointed out that, not only were the Administrative Class civil
servants amateurs but so were the Ministers they served. Lodge (2006) gave a
more-recent view:

> Whitehall has always prided itself on its ability to offer strong analytical
> policy advice to its political masters. Yet the almost exclusive focus on
> 'delivery' has meant significant problems in the way that policy is
> developed and managed in Whitehall [have been overlooked]. This is,
> in part, because consensus-building is inherent in Whitehall's culture,
> resulting in a tendency to produce policy which is timid and risk averse,
> often leading ministers to seek bolder thinking from outside bodies such
> as thinktanks and consultants.

Both documents call into question the efficacy of a system that relied upon
the analytical skills of highly-intelligent generalists, rather than technically-
qualified specialists. Specialists, however, may not be able to see the broader
wood for the trees and, when our body of knowledge is rapidly expanding,
may give yesterday's solution to today's problems. Although, in this view, the
civil servants are generalists, many of them have spent most of their working
lives in the defence field and are not without knowledge of its intricacies
and also that of the Whitehall 'system'. Despite many attempts by successive
governments to modernise this system (Fry 1981), the authors of the Trevelyan-
Northcote Report of 1856 may well have recognised some elements in the style

of operations in Whitehall in the twentieth century. Civil servants now have training in management, finance and technology but the basic method is still 'learning by doing'. Nonetheless, there was an attraction for a Defence Review that was open to inputs from whomsoever felt that they had something to say. Despite this openness, the analytical work in the Review would have to be done in the MoD by the staff which would have to implement its decisions and be endorsed by the political leaders who would bear the responsibility for any errors or misjudgements.

Since all the recent defence reviews had been dominated by the Treasury's demands to save money, there was a widespread apprehension that SDR would follow the same course. As late as November 1997, during the debate in the House of Lords several noble lords expressed this fear.

Lord Gilbert said:

> As your Lordships will know, this country has already received a substantial peace dividend since the end of the Cold War. Since the mid-1980s, defence expenditure in the United Kingdom has fallen by 29 per cent in real terms and now stands at 2.7 per cent of our GDP, which your Lordships may be surprised to know is the lowest level since the mid-1930s.

> (Hansard: Column 1485)

This view was echoed by Baroness Park of Monmouth:

> We already spend a lower percentage of GDP (2.7 per cent) than Greece or Turkey, let alone the US; less per capita than Norway, France, Denmark or the US; and less in actual expenditure than the US, France or Germany. Before Parliament returned from the Recess it was hardly reassuring to read in the Sunday Times of 12th October that the Treasury, 'intended to force the MoD into a huge disposal of land and other assets in order to finance its future equipment spending.

> (Hansard: Column 1510)

Mr Robertson, however, was adamant from the outset that SDR was to be foreign policy led. In reality, the staffs involved knew that a resulting defence policy, the costs of which did not keep within existing financial limits, or even show some savings from efficiency and cost-effectiveness, was bound to provoke powerful opposition from the Treasury. McInnes (1998:826) added that there was a further complication, 'the SDR became entangled in the Whitehall-wide Comprehensive Spending Review led by the Treasury. An early SDR would steal a march on the Comprehensive Spending Review and, from the Treasury perspective, might provide it with an unwelcome fait accompli.'

Patrick Wintour (1998) commented that Mr Robertson had to devise a structure for the Review that ensured that the heads of the three Services 'could not cook up some deal between them and present it as a *fait accompli.*' The power of the heads of the individual Services had been gradually eroded over the years, principally during the time that Lord Mountbatten was Chief of Defence Staff. The growth of the Central Staff lessened the independent management of the single Services but there still remained the possibility of 'side' deals being struck. As will be seen, this characteristic of governmental policy making, bargaining and the making of deals and trade-offs, has been recognised by Allison and Zelikow (1999) in their powerful analysis of the Cuban Missile Crisis of 1962.

The role of the MoD was to be the central, coordinating (not necessarily controlling) body in SDR and the Supporting Essays document, page 1 defined that Department's objectives:

- to produce a defence strategy, policy and programme matched to our security needs now and in the future;

- to help dispel hostility and to build and maintain trust through defence diplomacy and to play an effective and leading part in support of NATO, the Western European Union and the United Nations;

- to provide clear and timely strategic direction on the participation of UK forces in conflict prevention, crisis management and operations;

- to allocate available resources in a way which maximises military capability and other Departmental outputs;

- to encourage the competitive strengths of British defence suppliers and within the framework of the Government's arms sales policy, to support British defence exports.

The structure and processes to conduct the SDR needed to enable these objectives to be achieved. Routinely, defence matters are controlled by committees and Appendix 1 to this chapter shows the structure of the senior committees in this process. It may be helpful to the reader to have a picture of the higher organisation of the MoD and that can be found at Appendix 2 to this chapter.

The Civil Service staff, which had the responsibility for the details of the Review's structure and conduct, had gained valuable experience of such activities during recent internal defence reviews conducted under the previous government. They had, however, to add the further requirements imposed by the Secretary of State of which openness will have been the most difficult to introduce into the closed, secretive world of the MoD. Security precautions are necessary for safeguarding knowledge that could be of assistance to potential enemies, whose espionage activities were often targeted on the Ministry of Defence. This veil of secrecy had, in the view of journalists in particular, been used to prevent publication of information on failings in the system and its decisions. In SDR, however, even BBC cameras were allowed into the Ministry of Defence to make a documentary, entitled, 'A Paper War: inside Robertson's Defence Review', which was screened on 31st May 1998. Sir Richard Mottram (interview 12th June 2009) recalled objecting to some scenes that depicted discussions in which junior military and civilian staff were talking 'rubbish'. The BBC's rejoinder, however, was that their agreement did not exclude showing rubbish but if it was classified rubbish, it would be deleted. The film was shown as a part of the openness that Mr Robertson had insisted upon in his Foreword to the Supporting Essays document:

> Throughout the Review I have been determined to extend the principle of openness, to reflect this Government's commitment to open Government and to encourage informed debate on all aspects of our defence policy.

The Press, of course, showed considerable interest in SDR although their input at the time concerned the content of the Review, rather than the process that is the subject of this study. New Labour also held a fascination for journalists as Rawnsley (2001) shows. His book concentrated on the relationship between the Prime Minister and the Chancellor and barely mentions the SDR and George

Robertson. The exception is a brief discussion on page 159 in the context of New Labour's first budget, in which cash increases of £220 million and £500 million had been given to education and the health service respectively but in which the Chancellor was seeking to cut the defence budget. Rawnsley concludes that Brown was outgunned by a combination of the Chief of Defence Staff and the Secretary of State for Defence and his Minister for the Armed Forces. What Rawnsley does not record, however, is that the budget that emerged from the SDR process was cut by the Treasury by £2 billion, forcing unplanned savings.

The strategy and policy decided as a result of the SDR was intended to fit the United Kingdom's defence forces for the 'long term' and into the '21st Century (Mr Robertson's introduction to the Review White Paper, Cm 3999). This laudable intention, however, was going to be difficult to achieve, given the inherent uncertainty of the future. The Review would be, to a certain extent, future proofed by specifying the military's tasks in a generic, rather than specific, way. Thus, types of missions were used to calculate force structures, rather than trying to identify particular opponents. Nonetheless, the outcome could always be argued as either too much or too little, depending upon one's point of view or agenda.

The open, foreign policy led, SDR was a bold innovation that needed to succeed to show New Labour's commitment to defence. If everyone was to be given the chance to make an input, there was no guarantee that such comments would have an impact on the outcome of the Review. Special arrangements were made to secure informed inputs from eminent figures in such fields as defence and industry by the formation of a Panel of Experts, who made their contributions into the highest level of the SDR structure. Inputs at a lower level came from the team that went around units of the armed forces seeking the opinions of those actually involved in delivering defence. The bureaucratic structure for the conduct of SDR benefited from the experience of the officials who had conducted internal reviews for the previous Government and permitted control of a very complex and costly exercise. The outcome was the White Paper, Cm 3999 'The Strategic Defence Review' and the 'Supporting Essays' which presented the policy that emerged from a year of intense activity.

Appendix 1: Main Committee Structure

Main Committee Structure

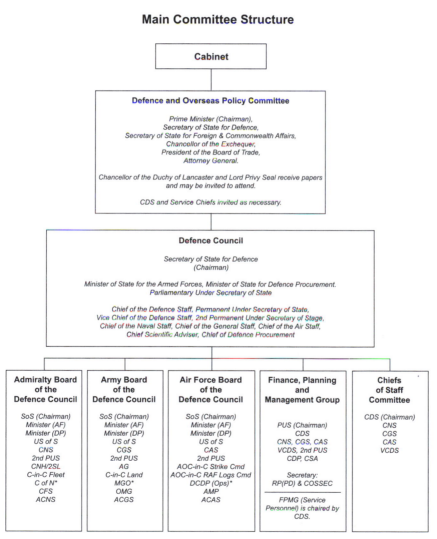

Source: Enclosure 82 D/DefPol/10/7/3

Appendix 2: The Higher Organisation of the Ministry of Defence

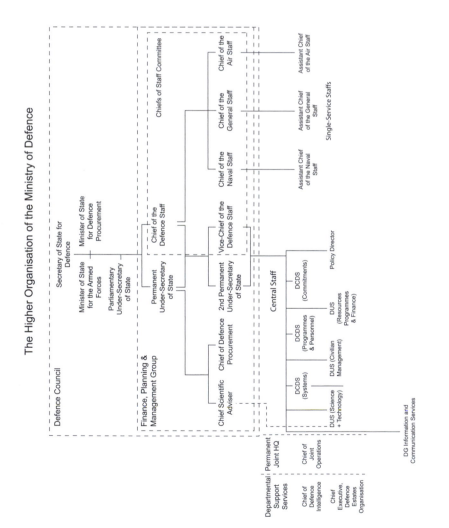

The Higher Organisation of the Ministry of Defence

2

Theories of Strategy

Introduction

Before considering what happened during the Strategic Defence Review (SDR), it is necessary to be clear what we mean by the term 'strategy', because this concept underpins the deliberations of the Review. This chapter briefly reviews the literature on the nature of strategy. Management science has devised a body of theory of strategy in the business context but much of that work is applicable to other uses of strategy, in this case, defence. Surprisingly, much less has been written about the nature of strategy in the defence context, perhaps because Clausewitz and Sun Tzu are considered to have covered it adequately. The subject was discussed in more depth in Grattan (2002) but some of the theory is revisited here to set the context for the SDR.

Origins

Grattan (2009b) suggested:

> Man's early existence would have been concerned with survival but, under the influence of technological and societal advances, he could, from a more secure base, begin to think into the future and to try to influence events, rather than merely react. Under the influence of what the Greeks termed pleonexia (wanting more), warfare developed and became a major stimulus for the adoption of strategic thinking, although this could not be achieved without the use of writing and mathematics to provide a cognitive framework.

Cummings (1995:23) placed the origins of our word in ancient Greece:

> *The word 'strategy' derives from the ancient Athenian title strategos,*
> *denoting a supreme commander of the Athenian armed forces. The*
> *position...combined the words* stratos *('army') and* agein *'(to lead')...*
> *The creation of the position of strategos reflected increasing military*
> *decision-making complexity. Warfare had evolved to the point at which*
> *winning sides relied no longer on the deeds of heroic individuals but*
> *on the coordination of many different units of fighting men in close*
> *formation.*

Sun Tzu wrote in the fourth century BC in China what is probably the first treatise on military strategy but now the term is in daily use. The full complexity of the concept is, however, not always fully grasped.

Some Semantics

The outcome of the Strategic Defence Review can be variously thought of as a strategy, a policy or a plan and we should be clear what is meant by these terms. The *New Shorter Oxford Dictionary* gives definitions:

Strategy   The art or skill of careful planning towards an advantage or a desired end.

Policy   A course of action or principle adopted or proposed by a government, party, individual, etc; any course of action adopted as advantageous or expedient.

Plan   A thought out arrangement or method for doing something.

Wikipedia has 'A policy is typically described as a deliberate plan of action to guide decisions and achieve rational outcome(s).'

It is clear that these are not watertight compartments in that each is defined in terms of the other. So a strategy is described as a plan and a policy is described as a course of action, in other words, a plan. There is, thus, a fuzzy area between the three that cannot be sharpened in a few words and the rest of the chapter may be needed to reduce the overlap, at least conceptually.

Strategy

Fundamentally, strategy is a series of measures adopted to achieve a stated aim. It follows, therefore, that one's aim has to be clearly stated. The conversation between the Cheshire Cat and Alice neatly sums up the need for an aim.

> *'Would you tell me, please, which way I ought to go from here?'*
>
> *'That depends a good deal on where you want to get to,' said the Cat.*
>
> *'I don't much care where –,' said Alice.*
>
> *'Then it doesn't matter which way you go,' said the Cat.*
>
> *(Carroll 1865:55)*

Thus, devising a good strategy for an inappropriate aim is not likely to prove very useful but often less time and effort is spent in deciding in clear terms what should be achieved than in working out the strategy. In sport, the aim is usually very clear – for instance, 'Win the World Cup' – but in business and defence the issues are not so clear. Set the aim too high in these fields and the resources available may be insufficient or may demand too high a proportion of national wealth. If those involved deem the aim to be unachievable, they may become demoralised. Setting the aim too low will not stretch the organisation to the results of which it is capable, as Hamel and Prahalad (1993) pointed out.

Mintzberg's Conceptual Framework

Mintzberg (1987) proposed the '5Ps' as a conceptual framework to consider the nature of strategy:

STRATEGY AS PLAN

'Strategy' is often considered as interchangeable with 'plan' since both are consciously intended courses of action. Mintzberg held that it follows that strategies have two essential characteristics:

- They are made in advance of the actions to which they apply.

- They are developed consciously and purposefully.

(In a different context, Mintzberg (1990:185) questioned the formulation-implementation dichotomy, principally on the grounds that those who devise the strategy are not the ones who implement it).

STRATEGY AS PLOY

The strategy may be intended as a manoeuvre to outwit an opponent. This idea goes back to a related word – stratagem. In this sense the object is to mislead by using an artful plan.

STRATEGY AS PATTERN

Mintzberg explained this idea as strategy as a pattern in a stream of actions, or consistency in behaviour, whether intended or not. The problem that can arise from this predictability is that an opponent can the more easily predict what course of action will be taken and devise a counter.

STRATEGY AS POSITION

In this definition, strategy is a means of locating an organisation in, and matching it to, its environment. In business terms (and this was Mintzberg's milieu) it meant finding a niche in a market where the available resources could be concentrated to the best advantage. Clausewitz (1832:229) gave similar advice when declaring, 'It thus follows that as many troops as possible should be brought into the engagement at the decisive point'. In real life, the niche and the decisive point have to be discovered by the strategist and are not always obvious.

STRATEGY AS PERSPECTIVE

Mintzberg explained this view of strategy as an ingrained way of perceiving the world. Hitler's strategies were conditioned by his view of many of his opponents as *untermenschen* who could not resist the superiority of the German race. Some companies seek competitive advantage through innovation, even introducing new products that damage the prospects of their existing ones, whilst others aim to win by increased productive efficiency. Strategy then arises from the company paradigm or their *Weltanschauung*: how they think the world works.

The Elements of Strategy

Pettigrew (1988) provided a valuable insight into the nature of strategy when he identified its three elements: process, content and context. The interaction of these three elements he illustrated by the diagram at Figure 2.1 and he argued that these were constituents of strategy and had to be considered together. They are like the dimensions of a box, where height, breadth and depth define the box adequately only when considered together. Although this book is about the strategy formulation process, it follows from Pettigrew's observation that content and context cannot be ignored.

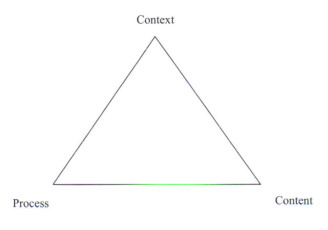

Figure 2.1   The Dimensions of Strategy

Strategy as a 'Wicked' Problem

Military strategy's concern is the totality of war, not the battle, and its scope is holistic or synoptic but even seemingly small factors may prove to be important and cannot be overlooked. The sheer complexity of this total view means that strategy formulation cannot be algorithmic, since at all stages judgement is needed in solving what Mason and Mitroff (1981), drawing on Rittel and Webber (1973), described as 'wicked' problems. Benign problems are ones that have a recognisable solution, such as those in engineering or mathematics, whereas wicked problems have no single 'correct' solution, they can be seen as symptoms of another problem and it is not always evident when the search for a solution should be ended. The problem of solving 'wicked' problems is compounded by what Liddell-Hart called the 'fog of war' and Clausewitz 'friction'. Some unforeseen event or difficulty can interfere with one's intentions and prevent the chosen strategy working as intended. Detailed, inflexible plans are most at risk from the unexpected and, when such occurs, the organisation relies upon its members to recover the situation. Bungay (2002:32) described the German Army's measures to counteract 'friction':

> *The German Army accepted that chaos could not be controlled but it still needed a command and control system. It adopted what it called 'Auftragstaktik' or 'mission command', developed from principles established by the German General Staff in the latter half of the nineteenth century, which themselves have their origins in the soul searching which followed the crushing defeat of the Prussian Army at Jena in 1806. The idea of mission command is that officers should understand their mission but be left free to decide for themselves how best to accomplish it. A 'mission' consisted of a task and a purpose. Both were articulated in simple terms by the senior commander but not specified in detail. Having understood the purpose behind their immediate task, the officers reporting to the commander were able to take decisions based on the situation as they found it but in line with their commander's overall intentions. This enabled them both to adapt to changing circumstances as the chaos of battle took hold and exploit unpredictable opportunities.*

Leaving such problem solving to the man on the spot has never been a trait in the British military and the problem is now compounded by improved communications. Satellite communications can connect the man on the spot with a distant headquarters which may take it upon itself to take decisions and issue orders which do not fully take into account the reality of the action in progress.

Strategy as Order Out of Chaos

Despite the problems caused by uncertainty, strategy can be seen as an attempt to rescue order from the disruption of 'friction'. The specific long-term future may be unknowable but the instability caused by chaos is bounded; self-organisation can generate a new order from chaos (*auftragstaktik*, for example); but chaos is a fundamental property of non-linear feedback systems, including organisations. The organisation is faced with the problem of creating meaning from the, often conflicting, evidence before it, before trying to impose some order on a highly complex situation. During the Cuban Missile Crisis, the Executive Committee formed by President Kennedy was faced with just such a problem and the first few days were spent in trying to understand Soviet motives and the strategic implications before they could begin to devise a response. May and Zelikow (2002) contained the transcripts of the audio tapes of these discussions, which make fascinating reading of the actions of talented individuals trying to find meaning and order in what seemed to be chaos.

Holistic

In the 1970s McKinsey & Co sought a model with which to analyse corporations and to reflect the pervasive nature of the strategy process. They devised the 'Seven 'S' model, which appears in both Pascale and Athos (1982) and Peters and Waterman (1982). The model contains seven elements, each of which is connected to the rest:

1. *Strategy*. Analysis of environment, competition, customer needs and one's own strengths and weaknesses leading to a plan or course of action which determines the allocation of a firm's scarce resources, over time, to reach identified goals.

2. *Structure*. Salient features of the organisation chart or a description of how the separate entities of an organisation are tied together, patterns of status and control.

3. *Systems*. Procedural reports and routine processes.

4. *Staff*. Characteristics of the major groupings of people within the firm by education, functional discipline of work background.

5. *Style*. Description of behavioural patterns or common traits of key managers and the organisation as a whole.

6. *Shared Values*. The significant meanings or central beliefs that an organisation imbues in its members

7. *Skills*. The one or two distinctive capabilities of the organisation which differentiate it.

The purpose of the model was to explore the interrelationships in the organisation and to discover if any element was dysfunctional which might account for any shortcoming in performance. The model is revisited in Chapter 8.

Strategy needs to comprehend the totality of the organisation's operations, taking into account the strengths and weaknesses of its various parts. Strategy making has been described as taking a 'helicopter view' of the organisation so that the totality can be understood and evaluated. Nonetheless, strategy can also be seen to be operating at and guiding operations at various levels. The Defence Review, for instance, did not consider a particular war but was set at a higher, more encompassing level, which is usually termed 'grand strategy'. Beneath this highest level, there is a hierarchy of strategies where the lowest levels have to fit into the next in the manner of a Russian *matryoski* doll. The levels, and their comparison from business strategy, are illustrated at Figure 2.2.

In Defence	**In Business**
Grand strategy	*Corporate strategy*
The application of national resources to achieve national policy objectives (including alliance or coalition objectives).	Corporate configuration – what is the business we are in?
Defence strategy	*Business strategy*
The application of military resources to help achieve grand strategic objectives.	Achieving competitive advantage – how do we compete?
Operational strategy	*Functional strategy*
Concerned with the direction of military resources to achieve military strategic objectives	Marketing, financial, technology, etc strategies

Figure 2.2   Levels of Strategy

Source: Defence definitions from Portillo (1997), Business from de Wit and Meyer (2004)

Grand strategy is thus more all-encompassing than defence strategy, which is one of its component parts. The definition above includes the concept of 'national policy objectives' which brings into play foreign policy, the level of national resources and the perception of the nation's place in the world and its alliances and structure. Figure 2.3 is a schematic diagram which suggests the sorts of influences that impinge on the formulation of grand strategy. The problem can be that these influences are not always specified and remain 'understood' and, thus, open to (mis)interpretation. The diagram does not purport to show how a national strategy is formed (if, indeed such a thing is actually composed) but rather how the ideas and factors involved probably link together.

Future Orientated

Strategy is essentially forward looking, which presents the problem of the uncertainty of the future. Forecasts often assume that current trends are projected forward at their current rates, because a change cannot be foreseen. Rapid changes do, however, occur and, for instance, the steep rise in the price of oil in 1975 and its sudden collapse in 2008 were not widely predicted, catching many unawares and negating their plans. Defence is not immune to the problems of prediction and the rapid collapse of the Soviet Union may have created a 'peace dividend' but it invalidated the assumptions on which our defence was based and left us with some inappropriate weapons systems. Defence always carries a legacy from the past and, given the length of the procurement cycles for many ships, aircraft and weapons, it is, like a super-tanker, relatively slow in responding to required changes of direction. Given the uncertainty of the future, it is prudent to make the defence strategy flexible enough to be capable of being modified if seemingly valid assumptions prove to be inaccurate. Such a requirement, however, will be very difficult to achieve, given that, for instance, weapons systems are designed to meet very specific objectives and resource limitations impose a limit on the number of eventualities that can be accommodated.

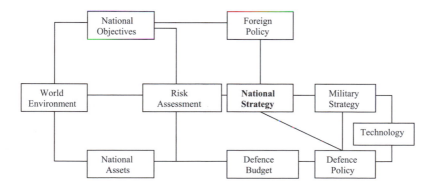

Figure 2.3   **An idealised model of how a national strategy might be formed**

Strategy as Mission/Vision

Strategy has an aim which defines 'winning' but vision is an imagining of a desirable future state and what that would mean to the organisation. For instance, the operations in Iraq were to overthrow the Saddam Hussein regime and stabilise the country's society. If this state of affairs could be achieved, Iraq could well become a stable democracy, sympathetic to the 'West' which would provide an assured supply of oil. Although the vision is usually created by the leader, Schoemaker (1992) defined strategic vision as 'the shared understanding of what the firm should be and how it must change', implying a link to the culture of the organisation. The United States and Britain both practised a form of democracy, so culturally it would seem an appropriate vision to replace the Saddam Hussein regime by a democratic state.

Each organisation has a set of values and norms that define and set limits to its behaviour and its strategy. Campbell and Yeung (1991) encapsulated this view in a model (the so-called Ashridge Model) which interlinked four elements: Purpose, Values, Behaviour Standards and Strategy. Their theory was that these four elements had to be in harmony for the enterprise to be successful. We have already seen the link between Purpose and Strategy, in that the latter defines how to achieve the former. Values, such as honesty and integrity, will form the basis of Behaviour Standards. As an example, whatever the commercial reasons for British Airways disposing of Go, there had to be a cultural and behavioural mismatch between a prestigious, long-range, worldwide airline and a cut-price, short range people carrier, which combination would have complicated the strategy formulation process. Kanter (1983:133) gave an example of the norms of an entrepreneurial company in which one manager described their approach as 'Ready, Fire, Aim' which contrasts with the more sedate, bureaucratic methods of the Ministry of Defence (although this is not to suggest that life within the Ministry is placid and restful). The culture of the British Armed forces is not entirely homogeneous: the culture, norms, values and behaviour are not the same in the three Services and so one can easily imagine that devising a single strategy for the whole of defence would present problems. The creation of a vision for defence as a whole, however, needs the holistic view described earlier and the purposes of defence are discussed later.

Strategy as Competition

A strategy might possibly be needed to tackle an unfavourable environment but most often one is needed to counter an opponent. Business is the search for competitive advantage and defence policy seeks to provide the means necessary to overcome possible opponents. In business, the opposition is generally known but, in defence policy, the type of conflict has to be imagined without necessarily identifying a specific enemy. Business seeks *sustained* competitive advantage but, in hyper-competitive markets, the period of success may be quite short. Defence, too, operates in a rapidly-changing world, where unexpected enemies may emerge or alliances fail and the available resources will never allow for worst-case scenarios. Defence policy, then, seeks the maximum flexibility to meet the unexpected and a balance of forces capable of undertaking the widest range of operations possible.

The Resource-Based View of Strategy

In recent years, a school of thought has emerged, based on extensive empirical research, which suggests that the competitive advantage of the firm depends on the resources it can command. These resources include tangible assets like capital but also, and importantly, intangibles such as competences and knowledge. Barney (1991:105) suggested that a resource must have the four following attributes to confer competitive advantage:

1.   It must be valuable, in the sense that it exploits opportunities and or neutralizes threats in a firm's environment.

2.   It must be rare among a firm's current and potential competition.

3.   It must be imperfectly imitable.

4.   There cannot be strategically equivalent substitutes for this resource that are valuable but neither rare or (*sic*) imperfectly imitable.

The atom bomb in 1945 conferred strategic (that is competitive) advantage on the United States of America, which was eroded when the Soviet Union was able to copy the technology. Pilkington Glass was able to protect by patents its competitive advantage gained through its unique float-glass technology but later found it advantageous to licence it to competitors. Resources, in the wider sense, underpin strategy when they meet Barney's criteria.

The specific competences that an organisation possesses can also be seen to confer competitive advantage. Prahalad and Hamel (1990:82) gave the definition:

> *Core competencies are the collective learning in the organization, especially how to coordinate diverse production skills and integrate multiple streams of technologies.*

The bowmen of England and Wales represented a skill that was difficult to imitate, was rare and strategically valuable and superior to the alternative, the crossbow. The archers were a core competence that ensured competitive advantage, until rendered obsolete by the introduction of gunpowder in the 16th Century. Honda's knowledge of engines and expertise in their production underpins their extensive product range and is the core competence that confers competitive advantage. Competences can be developed, as the British Army acquired the skills of counter-insurgency warfare in Northern Ireland but can also be lost if that proficiency is not maintained in training or actual operations. A further difficulty lies in identifying which are the organisation's core competences that are the basis for competitive advantage, since their significance may not always be readily evident. The evaluation of the existing competencies and the identification of gaps that need to be filled, form part of the process of strategy formulation. The environment is never static and a further difficulty is the acceptance that yesterday's core competence can become irrelevant in a changed situation.

Capabilities-based strategy

Capabilities are skills that can confer an advantage on their possessor, whilst competences are activities in which the company or organisation excels. The idea of capability-based strategy is a subset of the resource-based view described above, since capabilities are a resource from which competitive advantage can be gained. Stalk, Evans and Shulman (1992) argued that competitive advantage arose from the 'hard-to-imitate organisational capabilities that distinguish a company from its competitors in the eyes of the customers'.

The Taliban in Afghanistan did not have the capabilities necessary to conduct conventional battles against the coalition forces but they developed the capability of making and deploying Improvised Explosive Devices, which cause casualties and hamper the operations of the opposing forces in a way that is difficult to counter. These simple, unsophisticated weapons had a strategic impact.

Strategy and the Environment

All human activities are performed in a particular environment, which can be permissive or restrictive. Strategy is the way that the environment can be exploited to advantage or avoid damaging effects , so one of the early tools for strategic analysis was SWOT (Strengths, Weaknesses, Opportunities and Threats). In this model, Opportunities and Threats were to be found in the environment, whilst Strengths and Weaknesses were those of the organisation itself. Strategy can be seen to be the attempt of the organisation to fit into its environment, or in the terms used earlier, its context. The term 'fit' implies harmony but successful businesses have been built on a strategy that breaks the mould of accepted industry practice. Thus, Anita Roddick, the founder of the Body Shop, described her business formula as, 'I look at what the cosmetics trade is doing and walk in the opposite direction' (Campbell 1991:664). By the same token, copying another firm's strategy is likely only to be successful if that strategy can be performed better.

Strategy and Risk

Since strategy is constrained to look to the future, and what is to come remains unknown, there is an element of risk inherent in deciding on a strategy. The strategic analysis can be thoroughly rational and logical but it will contain the flaw that some of the data used will be forecast and thus uncertain. Some idea of the effects of this uncertainty can be gauged by conducting a sensitivity analysis, which will seek to show the effects of an error in selected parameters, and from this, an estimate of the risks involved. As we shall see in the next chapter, the uncertainty factor may encourage the strategist to think intuitively rather than rationally.

Summary

Hax (1990) summarised his concept of strategy in six dimensions, three of which are relevant to the SDR:

1. Strategy as a coherent, unifying and integrative pattern of decisions

2. Strategy as a means of establishing an organisation's purpose in terms of its long-term objectives

3. Strategy as a definition of a firm's competitive domain.

He stated, as we have seen, that strategy is holistic and related to the aims and purpose of the organisation. Strategic decisions create a pattern that is related to the purpose of the firm but also are an expression of its values and culture. Strategy is long-term and represents the means of achieving the vision of a future state that guides the organisation's aspirations. Strategy defines the environment that has been chosen for the firm's competitive activities and the means of securing long-term competitive advantage in that chosen *milieu*.

Rumelt (1980) produced a different set of properties of strategy:

*   *Consistency* The strategy must not present mutually inconsistent goals and policies.

*   *Consonance* The strategy must represent an adaptive response to the external environment and to the critical changes occurring within it.

*   *Advantage* The strategy must provide for the creation and/or maintenance of a competitive advantage in the selected area of activity.

*   *Feasibility* The strategy must neither overtax available resources nor create unsolvable subproblems.

In grand strategic terms, defining the environment establishes the likely types of opponents that are to be met and hence the resources needed; an approach adopted in the SDR. There remained, however, Rumelt's fourth factor which was entirely within the purview of the Treasury.

3

Theories of Strategy Formulation

Introduction

The way that strategy is formed can seem mysterious. James Brian Quinn (1978:96) recorded a response from an interviewee:

> *When I was younger I always conceived of a room where all these [strategic] concepts were worked out for the whole company. Later I didn't find any such room… The strategy [of the company] may not even exist in the mind of one man. I certainly don't know where it is written down. It is simply transmitted in the series of decisions made.*

> *(Interview quote)*

The first assumption here seemed to be that strategy is formulated by 'great men' having superior intellect thinking rationally in debate in smoke-filled rooms to determine some masterful plan to confound the enemy. This does not seem to be the case in real life. There is even doubt that strategy formulation is always rational and decisions may be reached either through an intuitive flash of inspiration or a well-tried heuristic. This chapter looks at theories of the strategy formulation as a framework against which to consider the process of the Strategic Defence Review (SDR).

Content, Context and Process

Figure 2.1 showed that the content, context and process of strategy are linked such that it is a mistake to consider one dimension in isolation. Pettigrew (1992:6) stated a principle to guide the study of strategy process:

> *...to abandon the intellectual trap now clearly evident in classifying*
> *strategy research into content and process domains.*

Thus, *what* is discussed influences *how* it is discussed and by whom.

In the same way, the process of the strategy formulation process is affected by context. The process, for instance, is different if the firm is facing a crisis because the decisions are taken quickly by the top management team with less involvement of middle management (Dutton 1993; Hermann 1963 and Papadakis *et al* 1999). If the team making the strategy is changed in composition, then the process will be different and the change may be radical, or only slight.

Process Theories

Mintzberg and Waters (1985) produced a diagram which is used here as a basis for Figure 3.1 to show the way that unscheduled and unimagined events can move the strategy determined by rational analysis (Deliberate Strategy) to a resultant (Realized Strategy). The idea of an 'emergent strategy' was an important counter to the ideas of the 1970s that strategy should be the result of a planned and rational process based on an empirical analysis. The 'Emergent' school argued that strategy formulation was much messier than that and, in any case, the 'bounded rationality' (Simon 1976) of the human brain could not encompass the fiendish complexity of strategic problems and could only devise 'satisficing' solutions that were the best that could be done, not the ultimate perfect result.

Furthermore, Mintberg and Waters suggested, some strategies that appeared to be a good idea at the time proved to be inappropriate and became 'unrealized'. Not only, then, do strategists have to devise the means to achieve an aim but they have to be able to recognise that what seemed to be good solutions can become overtaken by events and have to be abandoned. This, too, is a difficult judgement to make since persistence with the strategy might eventually lead to success, or rapid changes might be seen as dithering and uncertainty. Often, in practice, a 'drop dead' decision point is established and, if the results do not reach some defined criterion by a specific time, then the strategy is abandoned.

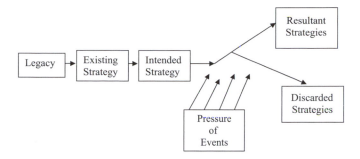

Figure 3.1 **Deliberate and Emergent Strategy (adapted from Mintzberg and Waters (1985))**

Incremental Formulation

This idea of strategy emerging can be linked to incremental process so favoured by government departments (Lindblom 1959). A large, radical step change in strategy is risky since it must involve a large number of unknowns. Small changes are less risky and will probably be more acceptable to the members of the organisation, many of whom would find large changes unsettling. If changes are to be incremental in nature, it is important to have a clear aim and vision of what the organisation is trying to achieve. Without this lodestar, strategy can veer unnoticed into policies that are suddenly realised to be undesirable. This behaviour is analogous to a story in the magazine '*The Week*' (5th September 2009:19) in which scientists studied volunteers walking through a dense wood. Those who took the test on a sunlit day, navigated by the sun and had little difficulty. Those walking on a cloudy day walked in full circles and the scientists attributed their waywardness to the accumulation of small random errors in the various sensory signals that provide information about walking direction.

James Brian Quinn (1989) proposed the concept of 'logical incrementalism' as a refinement of Lindblom's idea of 'muddling through' and as a challenge to the rational-analytical explanation of strategy formulation. He argued:

> *The full strategy is rarely written down in any one place. The processes used to arrive at the total strategy are typically fragmented, evolutionary and largely intuitive. Although one can usually find embedded in these fragments some very refined pieces of formal strategic analysis, the real strategy tends to evolve as internal decisions and external events flow*

together to create a new, widely shared consensus for action among key
members of the top management team.

(op cit 45)

Punctuated Equilibrium

Eldredge and Gould (1972) suggested that the evolution of species was characterised by long periods of stability punctuated by sudden change and then Baumgartner and Jones (1993) presented their model of punctuated equilibrium in the policy field. The latter model states that policy generally changes only incrementally due to several restraints, namely the stickiness or conservatism of institutional cultures, vested interests and the bounded rationality of the individuals concerned. This model resembles the pattern of defence policy formation traced in Chapter 5, which looks at the precursors of the Strategic Defence Review of 1997. In the main, defence policy does not change radically until some event, like the end of the Cold War, or deterioration in the nation's finances forces a rethink. The SDR was unusual in that respect in that New Labour wished to conduct a fundamental reappraisal of defence policy in the light of the foreign policy objectives, even though bounded rationality might introduce limitations and errors.

The Linear/Rational Model

The process named by Mintzberg (1990) as the 'Design School' arose from the work of the early theorists in strategic management, such as Andrews (1971) and Ansoff (1965). They posited that strategy could be formulated by a rational analysis of the external and internal environment of the firm and that decisions were made by the top management, the so-called 'dominant coalition'. In the 1970s, this idea was used by companies to establish a planning round in which a team gathered information from within and without the firm at the same time in each year and in successive stages prepared and refined the data for the board's decision, which again was taken in the same month each year. The process was lengthy and exhaustive but was unresponsive to the sudden changes that can occur. There resulted a tendency to suppress creativity and the flashes of intuition that could transform a pedestrian strategy into an innovative, winning one. Furthermore, Mintzberg criticised the idea that strategy could be formed entirely by the heads of the organisation who were necessarily remote from the day-to-day workings of the firm.

Mintzberg (1991) associated the form of the organisation and the strategy formulation process adopted as shown in Figure 3.2:

Organisational Form	Strategic Preoccupation
Entrepreneurial	The direction of the firm's development
Professional	Proficiency
Adhocracy	Innovation
Diversified	Concentration on distinct products and markets
Machine bureaucracy	Efficiency

Figure 3.2   Forms of organisation and strategic preoccupations

Thus, professional firms, such as architects, doctors and scientists, would see that their competitive advantage stemmed from the excellence of their work and were thus preoccupied with improving this aspect. The work of large, machine bureaucracies is difficult to control or even understand, which is why so many adopt the formalised strategy process of the 'Design School' type. The need for control is manifested in the imposition of rules, regulations and standards. The Ministry of Defence (MoD) is such a machine bureaucracy, where the size and widespread nature of its operations make control and intercommunication difficult.

Bower (1970) is an account of a research project which studied the resource allocation process in a large, diversified, American company. The interest here is that it describes a strategy-forming process and these ideas were taken up by Burgelman. The very large American corporation in which Bower studied the resource allocation process was multidivisional, multiproduct and multinational. The projects either had to be consistent with the strategy of the firm or they constituted a change in that strategy. He found that the attempt to spend vast sums of money on capital projects occupied a good deal of management time but no one manager could be assumed to have the knowledge or the time to handle the detailed programmes to use these funds. So the projects were initiated at working level but could only succeed if they were given support and 'impetus' by divisional heads. Corporate management made the final decision and rarely refused a project that was enthusiastically supported at the divisional level.

Burgelman (1983) made a distinction between activities that were within the firm's current concept of strategy and autonomous activities that were outside that concept. He found that the final strategy was a result of the 'stream of strategic behaviors at operational levels' (p. 66). However:

> Projects only survive if they receive impetus from divisional level management. This impetus process is highly political, because managers at the divisional level are aware that their career prospects depend, to a large extent, on developing a good 'batting average' in supporting strategic projects. Thus managers will evaluate proposals in the light of the reward and measurement systems that determine whether it is in their interest to provide impetus for a particular project. At the corporate level, the major contribution is precisely the manipulation of the structural context within which the proposal generation takes shape. Through the manipulation of structural context, top management can influence the type of proposals that will be defined and given impetus.

> (Burgelman 1983: p. 64)

The Bower-Burgelman model, then, saw strategy being developed by the activities at working level, filtered in the middle management and endorsed or rejected at the top levels of the firm.

Three Modes of Formulation

Chaffee (1985) described three modes of strategy formulation. Having genuflected in the direction of the rational model, she introduced the adaptive and interpretive (*sic*) models. The 'Adaptive' model saw strategy as a match between the opportunities and threats in the environment and the capabilities of the company (the familiar SWOT acronym). The third model suggested that members of the organisation collectively construct and agree upon their view of the nature of the external context, before devising ways of achieving the firm's goals. Although a useful taxonomy, Chaffee does not describe how these processes are accomplished.

The Garbage Can Model

There is a view that the concept of a formal process to strategy formulation is misleading and that, in common with many activities involving humans, it is messy and unstructured. Cohen *et al* (1972) suggested that organisations can be anarchical, at least for periods of time if not permanently, and are characterised by three general properties:

1.   The preferences of the organisation, which are more a loose collection of ideas than a coherent structure, are inconsistent and ill-defined.

2.   The processes of the organisation are not understood by its members, who operate on a simple trial and error basis.

3.   Participants vary in the amount of time and effort that they devote to different domains, so the boundaries of the organisation are uncertain.

If organisations are vehicles for problem-solving, bargaining and interpretation, then they can be seen as a coalition of choices looking for problems; issues and feelings looking for decision situations; solutions looking for issues to which they might be the answer; and decision-makers looking for work. Most of the 'garbage can' research, however, seems to have been conducted in universities and the model is hard to relate to the bureaucratic organisation of the MoD.

The Dominant Coalition

Strategy is the business of the top management team, although this does not mean that they alone formulate the strategy and it is suggested that they should be distanced from day-to-day operations for which the managers are responsible. The top management team is a coalition, often called the dominant coalition, which implies a degree of heterogeneity of knowledge, experience and expertise. These differences will probably result in individual paradigms that will clash with others and cause conflict. Power is shared but the strength of an individual's power will vary with the context and the subject under discussion. For instance, in considering budgets, the finance director may have an advantage through his expert power (Handy 1990) but the other directors will have sufficient knowledge of finance to challenge his or her opinions and judgements. Since issues of power are involved, the workings of this dominant coalition are political and alliances are likely to be formed and reformed in an attempt to accumulate the power necessary to establish the legitimacy of one's ideas and demands. The individual members, whilst working to achieve a common purpose, will have their own agenda and their own perception of the way to proceed, so differences are likely. In fact, such differences are beneficial to the strategy process since controversy questions the validity of arguments and the logic has to be sound to answer these challenges or it is rejected. The alternative of 'groupthink' where arguments are not challenged can lead to a sub-optimal decision process.

The dominant coalition in the SDR was not heterogeneous, being comprised of several groupings as shown in Figure 3.3. These groupings can be detected in the organisation diagram in Appendix 2 (Chapter 1). It may be argued that the Treasury were not partners in a coalition but an enemy. However, in terms of decision making, they were part of the team. Although every one of these groups was committed to producing a defence policy, they will have had their own view of what constituted an acceptable outcome and would have argued accordingly.

Ultimately, decision rested with the Cabinet but it only saw the resultant strategy, not the forces acting to form it. Many Cabinet members would not have understood the subtleties and fine details of the proposed strategy and would have had to rely upon commonsense appraisals.

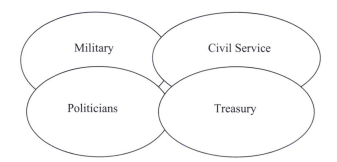

Figure 3.3   **The composition of the dominant coalition in SDR**

Strategy as Practice

A more recent change of focus in the study of strategy formulation is the work of the 'Strategy as Practice' school which criticises earlier process research for being 'primarily concerned with explanations at the firm level of analysis, necessarily sacrificing more fine-grained analyses of activity construction.' (Jarzabkowski 2005:3). This new approach investigates strategy formulation as a flow of organisational activity where the work of everybody is deemed to affect the resulting strategy. As such, 'Strategy as Practice' might be viewed principally as a research approach but it makes the point that the formulation process is fragmented and located in most parts of the organisation.

Allison and Zelikow

Much of the theorising on strategy formulation processes has been conducted in the context of strategic management: that is, in business. A notable exception is Graham Allison (1971), followed by the second edition by Graham Allison and Philip Zelikow (1999), which analysed the process of strategy formulation during the Cuban Missile Crisis of 1962. Admittedly, the context was one of a dangerous crisis but the involvement of politicians, the military and the civil service makes these events relevant to a study of the SDR, even though the latter was conducted in a more peaceful setting. Allison and Zelikow were concerned with frames of reference for the analysis of events in domestic and foreign policy formation and for gaining an understanding how these processes were actually conducted. The three models they produced can be seen as 'lenses' through which to view the events and the analyst is invited to select which of them gives the best explanation for the observed outcome. Importantly, the work also aimed at producing *predictive* models that could be used to forecast the outcome of the situation being analysed. The models had to cover all possibilities, even though the authors probably had doubts that, in particular, the Rational Actor model, though credible, could be used effectively in practice.

Interestingly, Allison and Zelikow suggested that their models could be applied beyond foreign policy to other situations, including business enterprises. This link supports the view that strategy, and strategy making, are human concepts and activities that have a universal application and the theories can be used in the study across conventional boundaries. Furthermore, they urge the analyst to use commonsense which, paradoxically, is not common and not use their models thoughtlessly.

MODEL 1: THE RATIONAL ACTOR MODEL

Allison and Zelikow (1999:4) observed:

> *Most analysts explain (and predict) behaviour of national governments in terms of one basic conceptual model; here entitled Rational Actor Model (RAM or Model 1). (Italics in the original)*

Since 'most' analysts use this model, Allison and Zelikow described it as the 'Classical Model' and suggested that it was based on the following assumptions:

> *Each assumes that what must be explained is an action, i.e. behaviour that reflects purpose or intention. Each assumes that the actor is a national government. Each assumes that the action is chosen as a calculated solution to a strategic problem. For each, explanation consists of showing what goal the government was pursuing when it acted and how the action was a reasonable choice, given the nation's objective.*

> *(op.cit p. 15)*

The SDR certainly had the purpose of producing a defence policy whose goals were determined by national foreign and security objectives. The government's goals were transparent and the whole process of SDR was an attempt to make reasonable and appropriate choices for force structures, equipment, etc. The one assumption of the model that is vulnerable is that the national government could be reasonably seen as a single actor. It will be seen that various constituents contended and they had their own agendas. Assuming a singularity covers further levels of activity that have to be uncovered if the process is to adequately explained.

MODEL 2: ORGANISATIONAL BEHAVIOUR

Allison and Zelikow introduced their discussion of this model, thus:

> But a government is not an individual... It is a vast conglomerate
> of loosely allied organisations, each with a substantial life of its own.
> Government leaders sit formally on top of this conglomerate. But
> governments perceive problems through organisational sensors....
> Governmental behaviour can therefore be understood, according to a
> second conceptual model, less as deliberate choices and more as outputs
> of large organisations functioning according to a standard pattern of
> behaviour.

> *(op cit. p. 143)*

Organisations are arrangements of individuals who combine to work systematically to achieve a particular purpose. Their combination enhances the individual skills contained within the organisation but the structure also constrains their behaviour. An organisation develops a distinctive culture of its own, which again affects the behaviour and performance of the individuals contained within it.

It might be argued that, in SDR, a special organisation was created for the purpose of conducting the review but those involved continued to perform their usual function and worked within the culture of the MoD. Rank and status continued to constrain behaviour, the performance of work using committees was a very familiar standard operating procedure and different parts of the organisation had their own agendas and objectives. In Model 1, the analysis would seek to be anthropomorphic and speak of 'Robertson' deciding the defence policy, where Model 2 would see the process as depending on the operation of the organisation to achieve a consensus by using its standard methods and procedures, even if there was a temporary restructuring for the SDR purpose. No single person was in control: the organisation worked to produce an answer acceptable to the dominant coalition who could then endorse the conclusions.

MODEL 3: THE GOVERNMENTAL POLITICS MODEL

Allison and Zelikow's third model is their most sophisticated and was introduced thus:

> The leaders who sit atop organisations are no monolith. Rather, each
> individual in this group is, in his or her own right, a player in a central,
> competitive game. The name of the game is politics: bargaining along

*regular circuits among players positioned hierarchically within the
government. Government behaviour can thus be understood according
to a third conceptual model, not as organisational outputs but as
results of bargaining games. Outcomes are formed, or deformed, by the
interaction of competing preferences.*

(op cit. 255)

These models were developed against a need to be able to analyse politico-
military events in the world but they are relevant to a study of strategy
formulation on a smaller stage. The quotation above can be viewed in the
context of SDR *within* a department, rather than in government as a whole.
The description here of the Allison and Zelikow analysis is mere thumbnail
sketches of a penetrating and elegant work arising from a study of the Cuban
Missile Crisis but a fuller use will be made of it in Chapter 6 when considering
the conduct of the SDR.

Policy Analysis

Friedman (1987:78) suggested that theories of policy analysis have been
strongly influenced by Herbert Simon (1976) who wrote on the behaviour
of large organisations which were trying to act rationally. Although policy
formation was affected by the availability of time, information and resources,
the greatest impediment was the bounded rationality of the participants.
Friedman observed:

> *The ideal-typical decision model applied by authors in the policy
> analysis tradition has seven identifiable 'stages':*
>
> - *Formulation of goals and objectives.*
> - *Identification and design of major alternatives for reaching the
>   goals identified within the given decision making situation.*
> - *Prediction of major sets of consequences that would be expected
>   to follow upon adoption of each alternative.*
> - *Evaluation of consequences in relation to desired objectives and
>   other imported values.*
> - *Decision based on information provided in the preceding steps.*
> - *Implementation of this decision through appropriate institutions.*

- *Feedback of actual program results and their assessment in the light of the new decision situation.*

Unsurprisingly, this model is very similar to other rational models as Figure 3.4 illustrates.

The Design School	Policy Analysis Model	Rational Actor Model
Leadership sets goals	Goals, Objectives	Objective
External appraisal		
Internal appraisal		
Creation of strategy	Identify options	Identify options
Evaluation of strategy	Evaluation of options	Consequences of options
Choice of strategy	Decision	Choice
Implementation	Implementation	Feedback

Figure 3.4   Comparison of three 'rational' process models

These models all approach strategy formation as a logical, controlled process under the control of top management, who are the only ones in possession of a synoptic view. The function of lower parts of the organisation in this model is to provide information. Mintzberg (1990) challenged this view and suggested that strategy formulation is a much messier business and that to exclude ideas arising 'bottom-up' was to miss the experience and knowledge of those who actually knew what was happening in the organisation. Grattan (2002) suggested that the process was iterative, with ideas circulating around the organisation, top down and bottom up, until the decision-makers at the top called a halt.

Summary of Process Theories

Figure 3.5, from Grattan (2002), suggests a family tree of strategy process models. The question this diagram raises is, 'Which one, if any, can be said to be correct?' The answer, although less than conclusive, is that, since none has been proved to be wrong, all contain a measure of truth and the one that is used in practice is dependent on many factors, such as the nature and purpose of the organisation, the personalities within the dominant coalition, the nature of the strategic situation and the contextual environmental factors.

Figure 3.5   A family tree of strategy process models

The strategy formulation process is context related. Factors such as the nature and form of the organisation, the external conditions pertaining at the time, the actors participating in the process and their individual paradigms, objectives and power, the resources available, whether the organisation faces a crisis or not and the constraints on the freedom of choice will all play a part in determining how it is done. So, which theory is the best explanation of the process observed is a matter of judgement and choice. Where the current level of theorising is less than adequate is that we are not yet at a stage where we can give prescriptive guidance to would-be strategists setting out to solve their problems. A justification of this present study is that, by describing what happened in SDR and relating these events to theory, it may inch us forward toward that desired goal but we have to accept that the conduct of the next strategic defence review may only resemble SDR in the task before it.

Planning and Strategy Formulation

Before leaving this consideration of the mechanics of strategy formulation, the place of planning will be briefly considered since a 'plan' is one concept of the nature of strategy.

One definition of planning in Friedman (1987:38) is that 'Planning attempts to link scientific and technical knowledge to actions in the public domain'. To many, the idea of strategy formulation and planning are inseparable, probably because strategy can be seen as having some of the attributes of a plan (Mintzberg 1987), at least in that it prescribes a course of action. The idea of planning arose in the 18th century from the belief that rationality and science could be employed in the study and reforming of society. Saint-Simon and

Comte worked to develop a body of theory and practice in this field in such works as Comte's 1822 work entitled 'Plan of scientific works necessary for the reorganisation of society' (Friedman 1987:70). The planner, as a 'Rational Actor' was deemed able, by using science and logic, to devise solutions for mankind's problem. There is, however, a fundamental problem to this theory. Plans are for the future: what use is a plan for something that has already happened? Science is concerned with the perfection of knowledge but there are no facts about the future, only assessments (or, more truthfully, intelligent guesses). Plans, then, are based upon assumptions and even their most rigorous, scientific development should not conceal this basic flaw. If the assumptions are correct, the plan may succeed, if not, adjustments will have to be made on the fly. If, then, we know the limitations and the potential unreliability of planning, why do we persist in making plans? After all, the Soviet Union placed its whole economy in the hands of planners.

Field Marshal Helmuth Graf von Moltke is quoted (Tsouras 2005) as saying 'Planning is everything – plans are nothing', indicating that the very act of planning is more useful than the outcome. A problem cannot be solved satisfactorily until it is properly understood and defined and the discipline of planning should lead to understanding through a consideration of what is known and what is likely. Planning is the instrument of change and has to be, therefore, teleological or purposive. As with strategy, the purpose of the plan has to be clearly defined and the likely outcome of the prescribed actions thought through. Given the uncertainties in the future, the plan should be made as future-proof as possible.

In foreign and military planning there is a potential difficulty in separating capabilities and intentions. During the Cold War, the Soviet Union maintained huge forces in Eastern Europe but their intentions were unclear. It seems that they had no intention of invading NATO territories but they had that option if they deemed it advantageous. The threat posed gave the Soviets some leverage in confrontations over Berlin and it limited the courses of action open to NATO. If a nation possesses nuclear weapons, there is not necessarily an intention to use them aggressively but the capability confers that option and with it, the doubt. Injecting doubt and uncertainty into the mind of a potential aggressor that he could achieve his aims forms the basis for the theory of deterrence.

A problem can arise, however, in that once the plan is made, the uncertainties and assumptions tend to be forgotten. Estimates may have been made using assigned probabilities but the chances of failure tend to be forgotten. Sensitivity analysis can help to alert operators to the weaker parts of the plan but what Clausewitz termed 'friction' will often appear in unexpected places to frustrate one's intentions. The outcome of SDR was a plan containing force structures, equipment plans and projected expenditure but the best hope was that the process had produced something that was 'about right' and not too brittle in the face of wrong assumptions.

In the military staff, a plan is usually constructed to show whether a proposed strategy is feasible. In the 1970s, when long-range planning was the vogue, it often seemed that companies would plan in the hope that a strategy would emerge from this work, rather than using planning as a means of validating a particular idea. Mintzberg (1994:22) commented:

> *Strategic planning should really have been labelled strategic programming, since it is a means to programme the consequences of strategies created in other ways, notably through the vision of a leader or the learning of people who take actions.*

The rational sequence would seem to be Decide Aim → Formulate Strategy → Plan and iterate around the last two actions until a feasible strategy is found. On the other hand, in chaotic, fast-moving, business situations, companies can adopt the Ready → Fire → Aim sequence observed by Kanter (1983),but conservative, bureaucratic bodies are averse to trial and error methods of this nature. In the case of defence, too much is at stake to run the risk of a total misreading of the situation through haste.

Summary

Theory has it that we should expect the large bureaucratic organisation of the MoD would adopt a formal, controlled process for the formation of strategy. In practice the yearly or biennial planning cycle continues broadly within the current strategic guidelines, making incremental changes, until the contradictions force a more formal review. Reviews, as we shall see in Chapter 5, are not always conducted from a need to correct a failing strategy and are often driven by the need to reduce costs. We would expect the dominant coalition to keep firm control of the process but there is still the possibility of flashes of intuition and insight from anywhere within the organisation. It is the nature of a hierarchy that much detailed work is done in the lower regions of the organisation, which is then endorsed or rejected by the upper regions. The top should have a more synoptic view, whereas those at the bottom know where the problems lie. The trick in strategy formulation is to be able to combine these two perspectives effectively.

4

Defence and Defence Policy

Introduction

The term 'defence' has become a portmanteau word whose meaning encompasses military operations and security, the defence of the realm and the exercise of political power internationally. Although it is the Ministry of Defence (MoD) in Britain that directs military preparations and operations, the Home Office is responsible for security, the Foreign Office, together with the Department for International Development, for international relations and the Treasury has control of the necessary finances. Devising a 'defence' strategy is, then, a complex, inter-Departmental exercise and the current Governmental structure may not be optimal in solving current security problems. Ashdown (2009) commented:

> This speaks to a wider problem with the government's current approach to national security, which has not adapted quickly enough to keep up with profound changes in the international security landscape since the end of the Cold War. In a world where climate change poses arguably a greater threat to our long-term security than terrorism or war, protection of our country can no longer be left solely to the Ministry of Defence. It now requires all government departments to coordinate their activities much more effectively and to move away from the stovepiped structures that inhibit an integrated and strategic approach.
>
> It also requires a fundamental change in the way we think about national security. Policy-making must encompass global, regional, national and local domains and better understand the roles that civil society, business, local communities, frontline professionals and citizens can play.

This chapter discusses the meaning and usage of the terms contained in the words 'defence' and 'security' in the context of the Strategic Defence Review (SDR).

Defence

Our word comes from the Latin *defendere*, which is defined in the *Cassell Latin Dictionary* as 'to repel, repulse, ward off, drive away'. The *Chambers 21st Century Dictionary* defines 'defence' as: 'The act of defending against attack; the method, means or equipment used to guard or protect against attack or when attacked; the armed forces of a country.'

These definitions, with the possible exception of the last, imply a passive approach to guarding one's possessions and that the defence of the homeland is the primary role of armed forces. Such, however, is not the whole story and so, before embarking on a study of the Strategic Defence Review of 1997–98, we should consider what is expected of this country's armed forces.

What is being Defended?

Britain has been invaded on at least two notable occasions: by the Romans in 43AD and the Normans in 1066AD. On both occasions the native population tried to 'repel, repulse, ward off, or drive away' the invaders, but without success. Throughout history, and around the world, indigenous peoples have defended their territories by whatever means they had available and such a use of armed force is not considered to be controversial. Currently, however, 'defence' has wider connotations, and armed force is not only used to guard the home land but is also employed to defend the nation's interests. This latter use of armed force is more abstract and open to interpretation but these interests are sometimes declared to be 'vital', which would imply that the power, influence or even the very existence of the state would be threatened by their loss. On the other hand, it might be, not our survival, but our prosperity or our influence in the world that is threatened. In the Cold War, our ideology was under threat and our armed forces were used to deter an attack on democracy by Communist forces which might have sought to bring about political change by force. We were assisted in that endeavour by allies, which might have increased the power available for defence but carried with it the need to agree our aims and our strategy with others.

These ideas of 'defence' are couched in historical terms and imply war by armed forces organised and equipped as agents of the state fighting an inter-state war. Such a threat to the United Kingdom is not currently evident but the 'security' threat from small groups or individual citizens has grown in recent years. These irregular combatants cannot easily be identified since they wear no uniform but they can terrorise the population and cause death and destruction in society using improvised and home-made weaponry. The MoD might provide forces to help combat such a threat but is not the principal agent for detecting and countering terrorists. Lord Ashdown, as quoted above, makes the point that this development necessitates changes to the organisation or practice of central government. If 'defence' and 'security' have merged, perhaps the MoD should become the Ministry of Security?

Defence and security, however, cannot be considered in the context of territory of the United Kingdom alone. Protecting our vital interests has an international dimension and so, currently, operations in Afghanistan are seen to be vital in the protection of the United Kingdom and its interests. Such a use of armed force in support of diplomacy has long been practised and the knowledge and judgement of the Foreign and Commonwealth Office is a necessary part of the identification of future threats of this nature. In the international context, defence is the handmaiden of foreign policy but so also is security policy. In the field of international relations, the United Kingdom is most likely to need to work with allies, since its power and capabilities have been eroded since the Empire has been abandoned. Operations such as the Falklands War are likely to be beyond the United Kingdom's capabilities in the future and, thus, the co-operation and approval of allies will remain essential.

The Report of the ippr Commission on National Security in the 21st Century draws attention to a further dimension to the problems of defence and security in overseas territories:

> It is also plain from the recent experience of Afghanistan and Iraq that the most difficult aspect of military intervention is seldom fighting the war but building the peace that follows. The UK and its allies have proved highly adept at fighting short, sharp 'digital wars' in swift order. But we have shown ourselves much less able to deliver a stable peace.

> (Ashdown 2009:48)

The need to consolidate the peace won by military operations is consonant with *Clausewitz'* dictum that war is a political act. The cessation of military operations does not signal the achievement of the purpose for which the war was fought. Failure fully to appreciate this linkage caused problems in Iraq when, after the fall of Saddam Hussain, it became evident that insufficient attention had been paid by the victors to planning the rebuilding of Iraqi society and its infrastructure.

In short, the term 'defence' can be used to mean a variety of things but a strategy cannot be defined unless the aims and intentions of the nation are clearly stated. In some circumstances, the potential enemy is clearly identified, but in others the threats are potential and there may not be unanimity within the country on the level of forces required. There may well be disagreement on what commitments the country should shoulder and these judgements can be related to our perceived position in the world. Supporting Essay 2, paragraph 5 stated:

> 5. Britain's place in the world is determined by our interests as a nation and as a leading member of the international community. The two are inextricably linked because our national interests have a vital international dimension.

This statement may reflect the foreign policy aspirations of Britain but it overlooks whether the resources are available to make these wishes a reality. The effect of this myopia on the process of the SDR will need to be considered later.

Although Britain can no longer be ranked as a super-power, we like to think that we are still a force on the world stage. Much depends, however, on the material resources of the country and how much of them should be committed to defence, as opposed to health services, education, etc. The diagram at Figure 2.3 is a schematic of the sort of interplay of factors that are at work in the formation of this view of our position in the world and from which should emerge a vision of Britain's place in world developments. Robin Cook, when Foreign Secretary, stressed the need for ethical policies but this aim did not survive the pressures of *realpolitik*, although the SDR documents did identify a role for British armed forces as 'being a force for good in the world'. The vision for the country may be shared in a general way but the measures for its achievement may not.

The defence policy adopted by a country is influenced by the national culture and its prevailing political ideology. Prussia in the 19th century has been described as an army that had a state, rather than a state that had an army, and militarism was the pervading culture at that time. Japan before the Second World War developed a society in which the military dominated politics and pursued an aggressive and adventurous foreign policy. The Soviet Union's ideology was that the capitalist world would collapse from its own contradictions but they were not averse to giving history some military assistance. America in the early part of the twentieth century was quite different and wished to busy itself with its own affairs and to ignore the outside world. Britain in the 19th century preoccupied itself with building and maintaining an empire and convinced itself that this endeavour was for the good of its subject people.

The revulsion deeply felt throughout the world at the events of the First World War led to a dimming of the 'experienced eye' and the adoption of measures that allowed Germany to cause the Second World War, so the prevailing culture is not always a good guide for defence policy. Politics offers a *credo* that may be selected by the public at election time and become the basis for the new government's policies. Socialism, as practised in Britain, is not a warlike creed and so the incoming Labour government in 1997 had to bear in mind the view of many of their supporters when devising their defence policy whilst facing the realities of the modern world. This dichotomy affected their choice of process for the SDR. Defence policy, like business strategy, is not produced *in vacuo* through a detached, philosophical process but must not offend the contemporary views of that part of society that cares about defence: a further constraint on an already complicated task.

Defence involves consideration of the interaction between nation-states and Miller (2003:126) stated the just terms in international law for this interchange:

> *States must abide by the treaties and other agreements they have made;*
> *they must respect one another's territorial integrity; they must not use*
> *force against another state except in self defence; and so on.*

The use of armed force has become constrained by the developments in international law and agreements, such as the concept of proportionality, which forbids action that exceeds that which is necessary to achieve the objective. This view conflicts with that proposed by Clausewitz (1832:84):

> *To introduce the principle of moderation into the theory of war itself*
> *would lead to logical absurdity.*

In practice, the application of force is guided by two Principles of War, the British version of which contains: Concentration of Force and Economy of Effort. Thus, the art of strategy and tactics is to concentrate one's efforts at the critical point and not disperse military force on non-essential tasks (an argument constantly deployed by Air Chief Marshal Sir Arthur Harris who led the British bomber offensive in the 1939–45 war). On the other hand, military forces must not be employed wastefully and in excess of that required to achieve one's purpose.

Defence forces also have the function of deterring potential aggressors. Theories of deterrence were endlessly discussed during the Cold War in the context of a nuclear exchange and became the subject of game theory, too. The basic idea is that a rational opponent will not attack if the consequences are that his losses will be prohibitive and in the case of nuclear war this meant the destruction of his own state. Deterrence operates, however, in conventional terms too and it was the judgement that Britain would not go to war over the loss of the Falklands Islands that prompted the Argentinean invasion (in this case a failure of deterrence). The level and capability of armed forces is a signal to the world of one's intentions, in that a country is unlikely to go to the expense of maintaining large military forces unless there is an intention to use them. There is a link, then, between defence policy and the perception that a country wishes to give to everyone else of its place in world and the roles it intends to perform. There may be an element of bluff in this posturing, which will become evident if this is called. The Suez campaign of 1956 is an example of political over-reaching and the Falklands War may well have had a different outcome without help from America. In each case, the armed forces picked up the bill.

Defence forces have to maintain the capability for meeting different threats and varying scenarios. British forces have not been involved recently in fighting in jungles, so should the country expend resources to maintain that capability? The idea has been studied that, in a stable alliance like NATO, countries might surrender a capability that others might take on. For instance, Britain might relinquish its air defence capability to Continental air forces in return for taking on maritime air operations for the rest of the Alliance. Leaving aside the question of the surrender of sovereignty and control over our airspace, such a decision would be difficult to restore if the idea proved to be unsatisfactory or the allies untrustworthy. The opposing argument is suggested by Sabin (1993: 279):

> If Britain seeks to remain Jack of all trades on a steadily diminishing defence budget, then the growing inefficiency of spreading its resources so thin may mean that it soon becomes master of none.

Government policy-making is generally incremental, rather than radical, as Lindblom (1959) observed. Making only small changes is less risky than achieving change in one large step but the difficulty with incrementalism is that it is too easy to lose sight of the objective and veer off track. It is possible, then, to arrive at an unintended and unsatisfactory destination and then a comprehensive review is required. Current events may divert attention by demanding a response which may fall outside the long-term requirements for defence. The Falklands War was an extraordinary example of the way that defence forces and industry can use existing resources to solve an unplanned problem but using this occurrence as a basis for future defence policy could well lead to undesirable conclusions. The incoming Government in 1997 decided that it was time for a pause in the incremental development conducted by the previous government and ordered the SDR.

Technology

Military effectiveness has depended on technology since the earliest times and inventions, such as the chariot, the longbow or gunpowder, have increased lethality and thus conferred a competitive advantage to the possessor. The Chief Scientific Advisor to the MoD in October 1997 contributed a discussion paper to the SDR in which he wrote:

> Technology has a far more profound effect on military affairs than simply the ability to acquire advanced weapons. It can open new modalities of war (such as information warfare), create new pressures on operational decisions (by the presence of the media in the zone of conflict), provide adversaries with instruments of large potential military advantage (such as biological weapons), revolutionise doctrine (such as manoeuvre warfare), challenge traditional command structures (through new communication concepts) and render inappropriate some of our tried and tested processes.

> *(Enclosure 12 MoD File D/DefPol/16/7/3)*

He made the important point that much of the technology used for defence is a product for the civilian market, particularly in information technology, but there is still a need for defence orientated research and development. In the 1980s this research was conducted in government establishments like the

Royal Aircraft Establishment and the Royal Signals and Radar Establishment. In April 1991, the Defence Research Agency (DRA) was formed which controlled:

- Admiralty Research Establishment

- Royal Armament Research and Development Agency

- Royal Aircraft Establishment

- Royal Signals and Radar Establishment.

The DRA was controlled by the MoD and continued until April 1995, when it became the Defence Evaluation and Research Agency (DERA), which also incorporated the Defence Operational Analysis Establishment and other minor research bodies like the Institute of Aviation Medicine. Late in the Strategic Defence Review, it was decided to privatise, that is sell, the DERA and a company, Qinetiq, was formed in 2001 to control the research establishments, although the MoD retained the Defence Science and Technology Laboratory (DSTL), which currently employs 3,500 scientists. Qinetiq is now quoted on the London Stock Exchange and also operates in the USA and Australia. The Ministry of Defence sold its remaining 18.9 per cent shareholding in 2008.

The Government now buys most of its research on the commercial market, although it retains, through DSTL, a capability in the sensitive areas of nuclear, chemical and biological warfare. Technology remains, however, critical to the effectiveness of the armed forces.

The Military/Industrial Complex

What has become known as the Military/Industrial Complex (MIC) is concerned with the political economy of defence. It is not an entity and has no formal organisation but its effect is sufficiently far reaching for the outgoing President Eisenhower, in his farewell address in 1961, to have warned of its power to influence the defence budget and even defence policy. Robert K Griffith, Jr in Koistinen (1980:1) defines the MIC as:

...the accepted process by which other institutions – notably the military, business and government – work together to provide the nation with the sinews of war.

The production of weapons has a national strategic implication, because interruptions of their supply may adversely affect the country's ability to wage war. An example of this problem can be found in Grattan (2009a:71):

As serious was the shortage of magnetos, since the source of supply before the war had been from Germany and stocks ran out in the summer of 1916. When manufacturers were set up in Britain, the need to import magnets, wire and insulating materials hampered production.

The ability of the Royal Flying Corps and Royal Naval Air Service to continue operations was found to be dependent on supplies of magnetos from the enemy, who, of course, took the opportunity to deny these essential pieces of equipment to *their* enemy. The supplier may be an ally but, still, difficulties can occur. If the purchasing nation is indulging in a campaign of which the supplying nation does not approve, excuses for interruption of deliveries can be manufactured to the prejudice of operations, at least in the shorter term. Governments, therefore, found it expedient to foster the maintenance of a domestic arms industry. Edwards (2009:11) made this point thus:

In a defence crisis, only national suppliers are 100 per cent reliable. Imports of vital military equipment are always vulnerable. What happens if the foreign policy of the supplying nation is not congruent with that of the buying nation? Sole-source 105mm ammunition from Belgium was, for example, denied to the UK in the Falklands War.

Commenting on the significance of arms manufacture in the late 20th century, Archer, Ferris, Herwig and Travers (2003:567) observed:

...military technology and production became a more important component of the world's economy than ever before in peacetime. The spin-offs from such activity often had critical significance – the technology used by the civilian airline industry is parasitical on the military sector, while until the late 1970s the development of the computer was shaped primarily by military requirements for ballistics

and code breaking. Since the major states preferred to maintain
indigenous sources of military equipment, while few could buy enough
of their own production to keep these industries afloat, the international
arms trade became a key export sector.

The Soviet Union was reputed to have devoted 33 per cent of its GDP to its
military (Archer *et al* (2003: 549) and it only used equipment produced by its
own industry, which was state-owned. By contrast, individual countries in the
West spent a considerably smaller proportion of their wealth on armaments,
traded systems between countries and the industries were privately owned.
Commercial companies need to make a profit to survive and the arms market
is very competitive. On the other hand, companies' research and development
effort is underpinned by Government agencies and launching finance for
an approved major project is usually supplied by the state, for subsequent
refunding. The United Kingdom benefited from the revenue from Defence
exports, which in the late 90s was estimated to be £5 billion per year, second
only to those of the United States (Rawnsley 2001:169). Defence exports were to
prove a difficulty in the context of Robin Cook's 'ethical foreign policy', which
formed the basis for the SDR (see sub-paragraph 'b' below).

There were strong tensions associated with the arms industry:

a)   Companies were anxious to sell to their own country, not only for
       the profit that accrued but also to underpin their export efforts. One
       of the first questions asked by a country considering importing
       British arms is whether the British government has bought this
       equipment. Without this endorsement, sales become very difficult,
       so arms companies lobby their governments to secure the necessary
       home sales first. Governments issue the specifications for weapons
       systems they require and companies liaise closely in this process to
       maximise their chances of winning a contract.

b)   Companies wished to export their successful products to maximise
       the return on their investment but the government were at pains
       to ensure that these weapons were not used for purposes that the
       British government did not approve. A case in point is the export of
       Hawk jets to Indonesia:

       On 17 July [1997], Cook made another preachy speech. Attached
       to it was a twelve-point plan, including a ban on the export of
       weapons 'with which regimes deny the demands of their people for

human rights'. Just eleven days later, slipping the announcement out as parliament was about to go on holiday and while Cook was out of the country, the Foreign Office confirmed that the arms would be allowed to go to Indonesia.

(Rawnsley 2001: 171)

c)   Governments, conscious of the financial, political and technological advantages of their defence purchases are under strong pressure from constituency Members of Parliament (and Congressmen and Senators in the United States) and indigenous firms not to import but to buy from local firms. The strategic importance of the defence industry is not overlooked in this lobbying. Britain, and to a certain extent the United States, are more ready to buy from overseas firms than many others, when the financial advantage is clear.

It had to be expected, therefore, that arms manufacturing companies would wish to influence in their favour the decisions of the SDR. The United Kingdom National Defence Association produced a report on 3rd March 2009 written by Tony Edwards, a distinguished industrialist, (Gardner 2009:31) perhaps anticipating a further Defence review, remarked:

The UK defence market has been opened up to all comers, sometimes rationally and sometimes viscerally because of the intense personal antagonism between the MoD and certain British-owned defence contractors.

He pointed out (*op cit:* 11) that the UK defence spending on equipment was split 68 per cent from UK-owned companies, 27 per cent from foreign-owned companies and 5 per cent from imports, whereas the corresponding figures for the United States of America were 91 per cent, 7 per cent and >2 per cent.

It follows that the procurement of defence equipment is a difficult and controversial activity. The MoD military staff produces operational requirements which are their future needs. Defining what is scientifically and technically feasible in the future requires advice from Defence scientific staff, the Defence Research and Evaluation Research Agency (DERA) or successors and also from the manufacturers who hope subsequently to win the supply contract. Inevitably there is technical risk in state-of-the-art technology which the manufacturers are reluctant to face alone and, in the past, contracts were let that paid the manufacturer their costs, plus a fixed profit. The MoD placed accounts staff on the manufacturer's premises to monitor what costs were assigned to the project but there was always the fear that the company was making too much profit. One retrospective assessment of the Bloodhound Surface to Air Missile system led to the Ferranti Company having to pay back a large sum of money to the Government. An alternative contracting system requires tendering companies to quote a fixed price and, in this case, the risks were borne by the manufacturer. In reality, the fixed price system had disadvantages, too, since it was to no one's advantage if unexpected problems forced the company into bankruptcy. On the other hand, manufacturers became adept at finding ways of raising the price of the contract. The performance of defence contracts continues to give difficulties, as pointed out in Supporting Essay 10 to the SDR:

> *Unfortunately, however, annual examination by the National Audit Office (NAO) of the top 25 equipment programmes led them to report that, despite the changes [in procurement methods], many major programmes suffer considerable time over-runs. Similarly, after some years of improving cost performance in the 1980s, recent NAO reports have recorded average overall cost over-runs of 7.5–8.5 per cent above original estimates ...*

As Edwards (2009) pointed out above, the relationship between MoD and manufacturer is often uneasy and beset with suspicion. Successive governments have not protected British firms by preferring supply from local manufacturers, despite many foreign firms receiving support from their governments, and have not impeded the takeover of local firms by foreign companies. The existing structure of Britain's defence industry may be a result of government policy, or an outcome of *laissez faire.*

If there are deficiencies in the equipment in use in the armed forces, rectification can be difficult. Lord Guthrie said (interview 13th July 2009):

> *One of the problems that arises in the defence budget is that you can put the little things right very quickly, but you can't put the big things right. So if you are short of protective vehicles or helicopters, you just can't magic them off the shelf. They just don't exist, they have to be built and you have to train pilots.*

Major, planned equipment programmes take many years to complete and the requirement may change several times during the development and production period. Eurofighter, now Typhoon, was originally conceived of as an air-superiority fighter in a Cold War context but the excellent airframe/engine combination has now been modified for strike operations, which has added to the project's cost. The A400M transport aircraft was discussed during SDR in 1997/98 when a wooden mock-up was available but the aircraft has still not flown in late 2009. The requirement for protective vehicles against the threat of Improvised Explosive Devices currently being experienced in Afghanistan is, again, a long term project that involves thorough testing and evaluation. Defence procurement is not easy.

The defence industry now has a European perspective and a number of collaborative ventures, such as Tornado and Eurofighter, have been successful. Integration, however, is not straightforward since different countries use different business models. The French defence industry, for instance, is effectively a branch of Government, rather than private companies as in Britain. The British companies, since their shares are available on the London Stock Exchange, are vulnerable to take over and several are now foreign owned. In 1996 OCCAR (*Organisation conjointe de cooperation en matière d'armament*) was formed from a Franco-German initiative and became a legal entity in 2001. All the current projects that it manages are being developed in France or Germany, although Italy is participating in a frigate programme. Progress towards a coordinated European defence industry is likely to be slow.

The Secretary of State for Defence, Mr Robertson, was aware of these pressures and he talked to the National Defence Industries Committee during SDR (Minutes of Evidence to the Select Committee on Defence, paragraph 101. See Annex B). The MoD were working on their procurement methods and intended to produce a revised procedure known as 'Smart Procurement' which aimed at quicker and cheaper means of purchasing equipment. Some of the problems associated with procurement were identified by Professor Trevor Taylor in his evidence to the Select Committee on Defence (his paper is reproduced at Annex C). Clearly the defence industry had to co-operate with this initiative.

Money

Defence is often likened to an insurance policy, where the premium, the defence budget, gives protection against specified risks. The dilemma is, however, what risks should be insured against, given that the necessary payment is usually grudgingly given, whether nationally or domestically. Strategy is affected by one's attitude to risk.

Defence costs money, a great deal of money, and it is only one of a range of activities that has to be funded by the Government. The Government itself makes no money and only has what it receives from citizens in taxes. Other competitors for government money (principally health, education, social security) are themselves large consumers of wealth, so the task for Government is to decide on priorities between the contending Departments of State and the Treasury makes those decisions, subject only to the views of the Prime Minister and the Cabinet.

A measure frequently used is that of the percentage of the Gross Domestic Product (GDP) and as Edwards (2009:4) observed:

> It is perhaps not surprising that there is a correlation between defence expenditure and GDP. The bigger the country in terms of wealth, the more it has to defend... The figure of 3 per cent GDP tends to separate the more serious from those who are less serious about the role of defence.

Following the decisions taken in the SDR, UK defence consumed in excess of 3 per cent GDP. It was decided that, in the years following 1998, the defence budget would be raised by a factor derived from the measurement of inflation given by the Retail Prices Index (RPI) rather than maintaining this percentage of GDP. RPI, however, is only one measurement of inflation and it is known that various activities and individuals have different rates related to their expenditure pattern and the nature of their purchases. Again, as Edwards (2009:16) pointed out:

> This explains why the Government claims that it has increased defence spending in 'real terms' whereas the armed forces know they have experienced effective cuts. The difference comes from the real rate of inflation in the defence world which overall is between 6–8 per cent, as compared with 2–5 per cent in the consumer world.... Defence spending reached a low point of 2.1 per cent GDP in 2002.

Professor Trevor Taylor from Shrivenham made a similar point in his submission to the Select Committee on Defence. The text of his paper is reproduced at Annex C.

The figures for 2007/08 given in Ashdown (2009:99) are:

Social protection	13.3% GDP
Health	7.3%
Education	5.6%
Transport	1.5%
National security	3.0–4.2% (depending on assumptions)

Defence, of course, has no 'right' to claim a particular share of GDP, which is why SDR based its policy on the needs of foreign policy but the budget resulting from that study was not approved by the Treasury. Different circumstances demand different defence budgets, so the 60 per cent GDP of 1945 reduced to 9 per cent by 1956 and to about 4 per cent during the Cold War. In this latter period, when expeditionary operations could be dangerous destabilisers of the political stalemate, expensive conventional forces were needed less than nuclear weapons (although these, too, were expensive).

When operations are undertaken, the resulting expenditure is usually largely covered from the Treasury reserve but there are always potential arguments as to what should come from the annual defence budget. The size of weapons' stockpiles held in reserve is difficult to predict since some ammunition and missiles have a finite life. Over-insurance can incur additional costs as, if the ammunition is not used, it may have to be scrapped. On the other hand, the ability and timescales to restock at short notice influences the level of reserves that should be maintained.

Money is a constant preoccupation in defence and the Treasury, given its role and responsibilities in the nation's affairs, are constantly trying to ensure that the MoD spends the minimum required. The arguments about what the nation can afford for defence are principally affected by the perceived threat to the nation and its interests which are generated, at least in part, by political considerations and public opinion. Critics accuse the Government of underfunding defence and Gardner (2009) quoting Edwards (2009) suggested that:

> *...Britain is not so much punching above its weight as 'punching above its budget – a far more difficult feat. (Italics in the original)*

Balance

New threats and commitments can arise quickly and looking into the future to identify emerging or likely threats can be extremely difficult. Contemporary operations have priority but this preoccupation carries the risk of distorting the balance of the defence forces. Gardener (2009:28) made the following assessment:

> *However, the reliance on continuously over-stretched UK military capability which is now firmly focussed on regional counter insurgency operations, has seriously hollowed out balanced defence capability and the resulting erosion of critical mass in key areas of defence is endangering long-term research and technology investment, making reliance on overseas suppliers (and a loss in defence sovereignty) inevitable.*

The operations in Kosovo were the last time that long-range, offensive strike aircraft were employed on operations and the current preoccupation with counter-insurgency, and the associated increased expenditure in that area, might lead to delays in up-dating such equipment. A similar problem might occur with anti-minelaying or air defence picket ships. The danger is that the balance in the armed forces might be disturbed by a current problem coupled with the perennial shortage of money.

A long-standing balance that has to be struck is that between nuclear and conventional forces. How much nuclear capability is necessary to deter a potential, nuclear-equipped aggressor? The possession of nuclear capability proliferated during the latter decades of the twentieth century and, although the Cold War has now ceased to be evident, the possibility of nuclear attack from some quarter or other cannot be ruled out.

Discussion

For the purposes of forming a strategy in defence, one needs to form a view, then, on the likelihood of the occurrence of various scenarios for at least ten years ahead. These uncertainties are so problematical that it is understandable that strategy, in business as well as in defence, becomes more short-term than is desirable in theory. In the face of stringent budget pressures, it may be deemed necessary, if undesirable, to reduce or eliminate capabilities such as anti-submarine forces, or tanks, or long range strike aircraft but once forgone, their re-introduction would be costly and would take a long time. On the other hand, which government would increase defence spending at the expense of, say, the National Health Service, education or welfare, unless a clear threat were to be identified?

Government policy proceeds incrementally, since small steps are less risky and can generally make problems go away. Heroic assumptions, too, can create the impression that a problem has been solved, when in truth it is only a short-term solution. It is too easy, however, to lose sight of the big picture and miss emerging trends that need long-term solutions. The equilibrium has to be punctuated by reviews that stand back and take a synoptic view and SDR was such a process. The American defence forces conduct Quadrennial Defence Reviews as a routine to avoid 'strategy creep', where as British experience pre-SDR was only to hold reviews when savings were demanded by the Treasury. Some are now suggesting reviews at regular, specified intervals.

5

Legacy and Precursors

Seldom is a human activity free of the legacy from that which has gone before. This continuity can be helpful as a guide but it can also be a constriction in the form of 'this is the way we do things here' and also the continuation of a commitment from the past. The very form of the organization can lead one into a process based upon its structure and its customs, that is, by using the procedures that already exist. A fundamental look at defence policy, as occurred in the Strategic Defence Review (SDR), is, then, a bold move.

Early Years

Society has needed and employed strategy from its earliest times (Grattan 2009b) and the formulation process was usually in the hands of the king or leader, perhaps with advice from elders. This centralizing tendency became marked during the time of the 'enlightened despots' of the 17th and 18th centuries (Johnson 1909). Louis XIV, for example, was not unwilling to listen to advice on military matters from such as Turenne, Condé and Vauban but he was, he thought, divinely appointed, with all the power that that status conferred. He made the decisions. An earlier example was Philip II of Spain (1556–98), who had a Council of key advisers, each of whom had direct access to him and Philip saw all letters that went out in his name, on some days as many as 400. Predictably, he became overwhelmed by the sheer volume of paper which passed through his hands. The quality of decisions and strategy depended too much on an individual and the degree to which he would accept advice and the quality of that advice.

The Eighth Report of the Parliamentary Select Committee on Defence (1998) contained a section on the Historical Context which was based on a submission by Stuart Testar (1997), although the original paper was not published. The report sought to trace the legacy of defence reviews and observed that these were undertaken either as a result of some military failure, or when it was deemed that a fundamental rethink was needed.

The first review that the Committee paper identified was the work that led to the formation of the New Model Army in 1645, a reform that was a result of criticisms by Parliament of the conduct of the Civil War. The forces of Parliament had been raised through county associations and some of the units were reluctant to operate outside their 'area'. Furthermore, the county associations were running short of money. Thus, in 1644, Parliament ordered the Committee of Both Kingdoms, a body which was responsible for the conduct of the war, to reform the army. The resulting New Model Army was victorious in the First Civil War in 1646. (Cromwell, who was then a lieutenant general was not a member of the Committee of Both Kingdoms). The New Model Army consisted of 22,000 soldiers in 11 regiments of cavalry, 12 regiments of infantry and one regiment of dragoons. (http//en.wikipedia.org/wiki/New_Model_ Army). This army was administered and victualled centrally, which improved efficiency. The army, despite the Self-Denying Ordinance, which decreed that army officers whilst serving could not be Members of Parliament, came to be a political force, which caused Parliament problems. Later, in 1688/89 the Bill of Rights established Parliamentary control over the army by decreeing that a standing army could only be maintained with its permission. Suspicion of the military and the standing army was to persist for centuries (even, some aver, to this day).

After the Glorious Revolution of 1688 and Pepys' reform of the Royal Navy, Britain's defence was dominated by the control of the seas but the threat of invasion did not entirely disappear, so the balance of spending between navy and army was a constant problem. Vagts (1959) described the power exerted by the nobility through their dominance in the military, leading to problems of civilian (and even royal) power over the army, which manifested itself in Britain as a struggle to control the budget and the command structure.

Nineteenth Century

After the victories of Trafalgar and Waterloo, the British armed forces were engaged for the next forty years mainly in small actions in the expanding Empire around the world. The Crimean and Boer Wars, however, revealed fundamental inadequacies in the army, which triggered reviews to discover what had gone wrong. The Stephen Commission of 1887 recommended a reassessment of defence spending on the basis of countering the threats, rather than what could be done on the money Parliament was willing to allow (Select Committee of Defence, Eighth Report (1998) para 18): an approach not common at the time. Edward Cardwell became Secretary of State for War in 1868 and set in train a series of reforms, largely arising from the shortcomings revealed in the Crimean War and the details are covered well in Jackson and Bramall (1992). Lord Carnarvon, Colonial Secretary 1874–80, headed a commission that studied imperial defence, and a Colonial Defence Committee existed briefly, with representation from the Admiralty, the War Office, Colonial Office and Treasury. The Hartington Commission of 1890 drew attention to the lack of dialogue between the Admiralty and the War Office and observed:

> ...*no combined plan of operations for the defence of the Empire in any given contingency has ever been worked out or decided upon by the two Departments.*

> *(Jackson and Bramall 1992:17)*

Reforms were made but, despite appointing a Chief of General Staff to replace the old Commander in Chief, political suspicions remained of the General Staff system and conscription of forces was not adopted. The suspicions of a large standing army and the struggle to maintain political control of the armed forces were issues that remained salient.

The Twentieth Century

In 1902, Arthur Balfour, the then Prime Minister, formed the Committee of Imperial Defence (CID) as a vehicle for the study of strategy at the highest level where the views of the navy, the army and the various government agencies concerned could be discussed and integrated. If this committee had functioned as intended, it would have provided a forum for the conduct of the First World War but its operations were severely impeded by struggles between the army and the navy, not the least over the choice between maritime or continental strategies. Balfour's government fell in 1905 and neither Campbell-Bannerman nor Asquith, his successors, really gave the CID proper support, nor did they seek to impose civilian views on the military. The Committee did do valuable work, not the least the production of the 'War Book' detailing the measures to be taken on declaration of war but it never performed properly its intended function as a forum for strategic debate.

The General Staff was created in 1904 as a result of Lord Esher's War Office (Reconstitution) Committee, following the failures evident in the Boer War and was only becoming at all effective when the war began and the brightest and best staff officers decamped to the Western Front, where several were killed. The General Staff in Britain had had a difficult birth but the system helped the army recover from the shortcomings exposed in the Boer War. The Staff had improved the army's relations with the Committee of Imperial Defence and had evolved the Continental commitment, which they considered to be a worthwhile role to replace the rather nebulous imperial policing role. Armed with doctrine such as the need to grasp and maintain the initiative in war and the principle of concentration of force at the decisive point, the Staff's task was to formulate military strategy for the British army. The assumption was that the General Staff was trained to reach the correct solution and that they would do so and without the tiresome necessity of coordinating their strategy with the other Allies

In 1906, the Secretary of State for War, Lord Haldane, presented to Parliament his first Army Estimates, which included the formation of the Territorial Army. He was in a position familiar to many of his successors in that he was cash limited to £30 million. He ruefully observed, 'If we had Army expenditure of £50 million to play with I could suggest many things that would be delightful and interesting'. (Howard 1970:84).

1914–18 War

The Army, now equipped with a General Staff, believed that it was its role to devise strategy and the Royal Navy had a similar outlook. The war, however, was of such a scale that it required the mobilisation of the whole nation: a situation that had not previously pertained. Marwick (1965) gave a detailed account of the radical, unprecedented steps, such as rationing, the direction of labour and the licensing laws, that had to be taken by the government to fit the country for total war. The military expected to be given the resources they deemed necessary to follow the strategy that they had devised. The two elements of society, the 'frocks' and the 'brasshats', were at loggerheads and consumed by mutual suspicion and incomprehension. Lloyd George (1936) is a full, but biased, account of the struggles between the military and the politicians and their failure to be able to discuss and devise a national strategy for the conduct of the war. A major disagreement was between the 'Westerners' and the 'Easterners': the former held that only on the Western front could a decisive victory be won, while the latter, appalled at the casualties, sought what Liddell Hart described as the strategy of the indirect approach. (Liddell Hart 1929). Since the Committee of Imperial Defence was supported neither by the military nor the politicians, the one body that might have resolved the situation remained powerless. Victory was achieved through the exhaustion of the Germans rather than through superior strategy.

Between the Wars

At the end of the war, Britain was exhausted physically, morally and financially. The Treasury demanded a reduction in defence expenditure from £604 million in 1919 to £103 million in 1922 and Lloyd George was determined to disband the newly-formed Royal Air Force as a part of the necessary savings. The Secretary of State for War and Air was Winston Churchill and, with the newly re-appointed Trenchard as Chief of the Air Staff, he contrived to continue its existence, despite the added opposition from the Admiralty and the War Office. Lord Haldane had been tasked to examine the post-war machinery of government and, although there was some support for the formation of a Ministry of Defence in some quarters, the proposal in the report for the resuscitation of the Committee of Imperial Defence, although without the provision of a supporting staff, was adopted.

In August 1919, the War Cabinet provided guidance to the individual Services in the form of what became known as the Ten Year Rule:

> It should be assumed for framing revised estimates, that the British Empire will not be engaged in any great war during the next ten years, and that no Expeditionary Forces is required for this purpose.

> (Jackson and Bramall 1992:118)

The guidance was intended for the estimates of 1919 but it became a rolling programme that was not finally rescinded until 1933. There was little scope for a defence review under such circumstances and defence policy was dominated by the Treasury's unwillingness to spend other than the minimum. The separate Chiefs of Staff could only fight over the scraps and internecine warfare was bitter and personal, principally over air power, but also capital ships. Events were to show that the Air Staff's claims for air power were exaggerated and the Navy's concentration on battleships, rather than aircraft carriers, was misguided.

In 1921, the Geddes Commission on National Expenditure began its work and the Navy and the Army renewed their attempts to rid themselves of the Air Ministry and to take control of the air forces relevant to their arms. The attempt failed but the Geddes recommendations on defence were less than satisfactory and Churchill was given the task of reviewing its findings. Geddes had recommended the formation of a Ministry of Defence but this large step was seen to involve many difficult problems and was quietly shelved.

In 1922, the Chanak crisis in Turkey required the Services to provide strategic advice to the Government but each produced plans that contradicted the others and showed no signs of any co-ordination. Again the shortcomings in the mechanism for devising national defence strategy became evident and the Bonar Law government appointed the Marquess of Salisbury to lead a special sub-committee of the Committee of Imperial Defence (CID) to study National and Imperial Defence. An important outcome of this study was the formation of the Chiefs of Staff Committee as a regular, rather than an ad-hoc, institution which became, under Maurice (later Lord) Hankey, the power centre of the CID. In 1926, the Joint Planning Sub-Committee, comprising the heads of the planning staffs of the three Services, was formed and, when joined in 1936 by the Joint Intelligence Sub-Committee, provided in effect the joint general staff that was to prove so effective in the coming war. The Chiefs of Staff made some progress in integrating their views into a national policy and began to issue an annual Chiefs of Staff Annual Review which listed priorities, matched resources and commitments and determine force levels. Some degree of unity of view had to be displayed but there was often blood on the carpet in the committee room.

The false comfort of the Ten Year Rule was increasingly being exposed by the deteriorating international situation and the 1932 Chiefs' Review called for its abandonment. In 1933, the alarm at the turn of events increased and a Defence Requirements Sub-Committee (DRC) was formed to manage a re-armament programme funded by the limited amount of money that the Treasury made available. This committee comprised: the three Chiefs of Staff; representatives from the Foreign Office and the Treasury; and was chaired by Maurice Hankey. The seriousness of the threat and the composition of the COS Committee, which had changed to include less-abrasive characters, led to more unity of view, but controversial issues and fights for a share of the budget still bedevilled the attempts to provide a coherent defence policy. If rearmament was slow and uncertain, the growth of the bureaucracy was not and in 1936 the CID had 68 military and civilian committees and sub-committees (Ismay

1960:78). The DRC produced a Deficiency Programme with an estimated cost of £75 million over five years but Chamberlain, the Chancellor of the Exchequer, deemed this bill too large, needing a reappraisal of priorities and proclaimed Germany, rather than Japan, as the main threat and the chief danger was from German air attack. These essays in strategy do not seem to have been debated with the CID.

In these nervous years the idea of a Ministry of Defence re-emerged as a means of solving the problem of inter-Service rivalry but the Prime Minister, Stanley Baldwin compromised by creating a Minister for the Co-ordination of Defence in 1936. The first incumbent was Sir Thomas Inskip. The Third DRC Report was used in 1937 as the basis for formulating defence policy, the structure of which review was to be come familiar in years to come. Jackson and Bramall (1992: 163) commented:

> *A process very similar to a modern Defence Review was set in train: the Treasury set the financial ceiling; the Service departments presented costings of their programmes for five years…; the Chiefs under Inskip's chairmanship determined priorities from their points of view; and the Cabinet was left to accept or reject the strategic implications.*

This period of uncertainty and hesitancy was ended by Britain's declaration of war on Germany on 1st September 1939

1939–45

The formulation process leading to a defence strategy in the Second World War is a special case in that the war aim was not in doubt and provided a unity of purpose not always achievable in peacetime. The Chiefs of Staff Committee came into its own and operated effectively under the Chairmanship of General (later Lord) Alanbrooke, and we are fortunate to have his forthright account in Danchev and Todman (2001). His relationship with the Prime Minister (who was also Minister of Defence) was not easy but the system worked so well that it was adopted first by the Americans and then as the model for the Combined Chiefs of Staff. The British strategic view was eroded as the war progressed as the American contribution became dominant but the process for the formulation of that view worked well under Alanbrooke – 'The Master of Strategy' (inscription on the plinth of his statue outside the MoD in Whitehall).

Whilst Churchill's influence was pervasive and dominating, he never over-rode a Chiefs of Staff decision on military matters.

After 1945

Britain ended the 1939–1945 War on the winning side but was not amongst those who gained the most, which were the United States of America and the Soviet Union. Although both of these had lost large numbers of men and much materiel, the Soviet Union dominated Eastern Europe and the United States of America had developed its aircraft and shipbuilding industries, had possession of nuclear weapons and enjoyed the technology benefits of the Alliance, such as radar and jet engines. Britain, by contrast, was heavily in debt and had suffered considerable damage to its infrastructure from bombing. Britain had been in decline since the 1890s and fighting for the whole of two World Wars (a degree of involvement shared only by Germany) had consumed most of its wealth and left it with industries desperately in need of modernisation. In 1945, Britain's Empire was more a liability than an asset, although the United Kingdom had received massive support from it during the War and the granting of independence to India and Pakistan in 1947 removed much of the logic behind its other possessions, many of which had been acquired to guard the communications to the Indian sub-continent.

Nonetheless, Britain retained a 'place in the world' to which it had become accustomed during its many years of prosperity and still maintained symbols of greatness, such a place as a Permanent Member of the United Nations Security Council. Successive Governments showed few signs of being willing to forgo this 'Great Power' status, even though its justification became increasingly questionable. Defence capability was a part of this status and, in any event, armed force was still necessary for policing in her remaining overseas possessions. British forces were seldom out of action somewhere in world (Palestine, Malaysia, Korea, Northern Rhodesia, Kenya, Cyprus, Northern Ireland, Brunei, Aden, Kuwait, all come to mind) and, following the formation of the North Atlantic Treaty Organisation (NATO) in 1949, she became heavily involved what became known as the 'Cold War'.

The period following the end of the Second World War showed, in Britain, the following tendencies:

- Economic decline and fiscal bankruptcy.

- Gradual erosion of the country's position in the world, despite efforts to the contrary.

- Pressure on defence from expensive technological advances, decline in its share of the nation's Gross National Product and overstretch of personnel and resources.

- Change in the governance of Britain and defence. The individual Services lost power to increased centralisation of decision and control.

1945–1956

Defence strategy and military policy was still generated by the Chiefs of Staff Committee system that had worked so well during the War. They evolved the Three Pillars military policy:

- Protecting the United Kingdom;

- Maintaining vital sea communications;

- Securing the Middle East as a defensive and striking base against the Soviet Union (Ovendale 1994:18).

The Cabinet endorsed this policy and the Foreign Secretary, Ernest Bevin, in particular supported the salience of the Middle East to Britain.

The Defence White Paper of 1946 (Cmnd 6923) created the MoD but the single Services retained their Ministers, budgets and direct access to the Cabinet, so the MoD had limitations to his powers.

The Chiefs of Staff had been convinced that Britain should not fight again on the Continent but the formation of the North Atlantic Treaty Organisation in 1949 and Britain's prominent role, forced a change of view. The Government were convinced that Britain should develop and deploy nuclear weapons and so decided in 1947. In 1952, the prevention of world war by nuclear deterrence strategy had become Britain's prime defence objective. The priorities had become: hot war in Europe first; followed by the Middle East and the Far East.

These developments in defence policy had come about through the reaction of the Chiefs of Staff to world-wide developments. There does not appear to have been an event which can be classified as a 'review'. In Jackson and Bramall's (1992) detailed account of this period, they observed:

> Changes in Defence policy rarely occur overnight. There has to be a convergence of ideas or pressures before a consensus for change builds up in Whitehall and Westminster. It often takes a specific event to focus the image of the change that is needed.

> (Jackson and Bramall 1992:281)

An event was about to occur.

1956–64

In 1956, the Egyptian government led by Gamel Abdul Nasser nationalised the Suez Canal. Britain had always regarded the Suez Canal as vital to access to India and the Far East and so regarded this move as a strategic threat. Furthermore, the Prime Minister, Sir Anthony Eden, had witnessed at first hand the results of the appeasement of Hitler and so firmly held the view that dictators must be challenged and opposed. These circumstances led to the last spasm of Imperial Britain, when the French and British, with Israeli collusion, invaded Egypt with the aim of regaining control of the Canal. In the event, the operations were strongly opposed by America whose pressure was such that a cease-fire was called before complete Anglo-French success had been achieved and the Canal was blocked by scuttled ships. A by-product of the Suez invasion was that the world's eyes were diverted from the brutal suppression of the uprising in Hungary by Soviet troops.

Sir Oliver Franks (in Fry 1981:119) commented:

> After the war we acted as a Great Power, though we had not the resources. A kind of confidence trick. It came off as long as the decisions we made were acceptable to the other Powers. The trouble with these island empires has always been the same: they had too few men.

He might have added 'and resources'. Britain had been humiliated and could no longer have a military strategy completely independent of its allies.

At this time, only America and the Soviet Union had that luxury and so Britain needed to devise a realistic military posture appropriate to its reduced circumstances, both economic and strategic.

Harold Macmillan took over the office of Prime Minister in January 1957 and he faced the need to restore the economy and repair Anglo-American relations. A revised defence policy was a vital part of achieving these aims and the task of devising a new strategy fell to Duncan Sandys, the Minister of Defence, who was judged to have the determination necessary to drive through measures unpopular with the Service Chiefs.

The Sandys Review was conducted by the principal civil servants in the small Ministry of Defence and with Air Chief Marshal Sir William Dickson who was Chief Staff Officer to the Minister of Defence and Chairman of the Chiefs of Staff Committee. Jackson and Bramall (1992:316) recorded:

> Such meeting as he had with the Chiefs [of Staff of the three Services]
> were acrimonious and confirmed their worst forebodings about the
> part he was going to play in their affairs. It was not so much the
> scant attention he paid to their views in committee that riled them,
> but the unconstitutional way in which he disregarded their corporate
> responsibilities for advising the Cabinet on strategic policy. He took such
> advice as he needed from his own small group of advisers at Storey's
> Gate, whom he allowed to usurp the proper functions of the Chiefs.

The detailed, and controversial, measures dictated by the resulting Defence White Paper (which had gone through thirteen 'final' drafts) are not the concern of this study, but they included ending National Service, putting greater emphasis on nuclear weapons and missiles and building quick reaction forces. The process of the review was centrally controlled and excluded advice from other than a small number of advisers so was almost completely top down.

The process of the Sandys Review reflected an underlying move to form a Central Ministry of Defence to which the three Services were to be subordinate, perhaps an idea based on Hobbes' insight that without an overarching authority an organisation is anarchic. This proposed reorganisation had the support of the Prime Minister and was pursued by Earl Mountbatten, who was then First Sea Lord but who was later to become the first Chief of Defence Staff. The Chiefs of Staff had negotiated defence strategy largely on the advice of their own staffs, so the result was usually a compromise, which made a radical solution virtually impossible. Would, however, Earl Mountbatten, if given executive power as CDS, have approved radical cuts to the Royal Navy if the logic had so demanded? As long as an executive CDS was a serving military man the 'fair shares for all' approach was in jeopardy. The moves toward strengthening the 'centre' progressed until confirmed by the passing of the Ministry of Defence Act in 1964, which after an internal review of the defence organisation, created a small but integrated MoD Central Staff.

After a General Election in 1964, a Labour government was formed and Denis Healey became Secretary of State for Defence. The Select Defence Committee, Eighth Report (1998), paragraph 24 recorded:

> *The Healey Review was, in essence, a series of separate studies undertaken by different bodies using different methods. It initially reported to Parliament in a White Paper of February 1966, (Cmnd 2901 The Defence Review) but was not completed until mid-1967. The process did involve a review of foreign commitments, but that followed after the decisions to make substantial savings by cancelling major equipment orders and reorganising and reducing the Territorial Army.... Although the 1967 White Paper announced continuing commitments East of Suez (though with 40,000, at half the previous manpower levels), it warned:*

> *Defence policy can never be static... This Statement...describes the framework of policy within which further decisions will be taken in the years ahead.*

Jackson and Bramall (1992:364) contrasted the 'opinionated one-man band approach of Sandys with that of Healey, who carefully examined and argued through every proposal with the Chiefs, the Permanent Under-Secretary and the Chief Adviser (Projects and Research)'. Developments in the political and economic environment forced changes to the original work started in 1964 and progressive withdrawals from overseas bases culminated in the final revision in 1967, which brought about the abandonment of bases East of Suez.

Roy Mason replaced Denis Healey as Secretary of State for Defence but the position was made unenviable by the appointment of Healey as Chancellor of the Exchequer who ordered the reduction of the defence budget from 5.5 per cent to 4.5 (or even 4) per cent of the Gross Domestic Product over a ten-year period. A further review became inevitable but the intention to base it upon a reappraisal of Britain's defence commitments was pre-empted by the Chancellor's dictum. The priorities the review established were: NATO's front line forces in Germany; anti-submarine forces in the Eastern Atlantic; and home defence, which precluded maintaining mobile forces and reinforcement capabilities.

In the second Thatcher administration, John (later Sir John) Nott became Secretary of State for Defence and faced the daunting task of rebalancing the funds available for Defence with the agreed equipment programmes. He quickly formed the view that the current plans were unsustainable and decided that a further review was necessary. The Army and the Air Force cases were made on definable tasks within NATO but the Navy did not have such evident roles. The Chiefs of Staff did not have a unified view on the measures required and the Central Staffs were not powerful enough to impose a solution. When the Minister for the Navy was sacked for releasing details of the proposed cuts to the Navy, the Prime Minister decided to abolish the posts of the three single-Service ministers, partly because the power of the centre in the MoD had been eroded since the Mountbatten era. In the 1981 White Paper, *The Way Forward*, the Navy was to bear the brunt of the economies, losing 'around' 15 frigates, one aircraft carrier and three nuclear submarines. In 1982, the Falklands War erupted and the irony that the British effort required strong naval forces was not lost on the MoD, particularly in the Navy Department. Fortunately, the proposed cuts to the fleet had not yet taken effect.

The perennial struggle between a maritime basis for British strategy and the Continental commitment had been swinging, pendulum-like, for centuries and, although the commitment to NATO had been given priority, the maritime case had reappeared. The Falklands War had also shown how brittle policies could be in the face of the unexpected. Cmnd 8758 (1982:15) stated:

> *The Falklands campaign was in many respects unique. We must be cautious, therefore, in deciding which lessons of the campaign are relevant in the United Kingdom's main defence priority – our role within NATO against the threat from the Soviet Union and her allies.*

So here was a dilemma: how much of the experiences in the Falklands should be built into British defence policy? Was the campaign a one-off, or a contingency that needed provision for the future? Some quarters wanted a further Defence Review and the Third Report (Session 1984–1985) of the Select Committee on Defence commented:

A likely consequence is that important issues will be decided as a result of short-term financial considerations and not in the context of a long-term view of defence requirements or by weighing priorities in a sensible manner. We are told that there is no immediate need for a major defence review, but we fear that the cumulative effect of managing the defence budget in the manner endorsed in the White Paper may result in a defence review by stealth.

(Paragraph 36)

Studies within the MoD had not ceased in this period but they had not the character of a fundamental, root and branch review until Tom King, as Secretary of State for Defence, conducted the 'Options for Change' exercise in 1990. The trigger will have been the collapse of the Soviet Union and the Warsaw Pact in 1989, which called into question the large British commitment to NATO, thus the deployment of large forces on the Continent and a desire to reap a 'peace dividend' in financial savings. Mottram (1991:25) commented on the processes involved in Options for Change:

Essentially, the exercise was run at three levels: at the top, close ministerial control by the Secretary of State and his colleagues; a central group comprising all the top management, including single-service Chiefs of Staff, which looked at emerging proposals on their way to ministers; and a small working group of central policy and programme staffs. This approach was designed to ensure close central direction and a defence-wide approach, and to allow for radical options to be addressed on their merits in private, rather than in the newspapers. Inevitably it had drawbacks and was not popular with those excluded or half-included. Inevitably too the results had to be broad-based and subject to detailed follow-on work. But it worked. In so far as the 'Options for Change' exercise was seen by some as a test of the post-1984 organisation, that test was passed.

Sir Richard Mottram commented (interview 12 June 2009) that the experience gained in the conduct of 'Options for Change' proved to be very useful in structuring the later SDR, although the latter was open to comment from outside the Ministry of Defence throughout. He also recalled that 'the single-Service Chiefs were very influential, but the myth was that it was a highly-centralised thing.' Richard Hatfield (interview 20 April 2009) stressed the importance of the 'Options for Change' as a precursor of SDR and the subsequent 'Front Line First' exercise, both of which had been conducted by Richard Mottram and provided valuable experience for the methodology to be adopted in SDR.

The result of the 'Options for Change' exercise was a reduction in the UK defence forces of 45,000 men and women, leaving 120,000 in the Regular Army, 60,000 in the Royal Navy/Royal Marines and 75,000 in the Royal Air Force (Ovendale 1994:187). 'Front Line First' in 1994 made £2 billion of savings over a three-year period and cut 18,700 jobs: 7,100 civilian, 7,500 Royal Air Force, 2,200 Army and 1,900 Royal Navy posts. Richard Hatfield suggested (interview 20 April 2009) that the rationale of the latter exercise was, 'deliver us exactly what you're planning to do at the moment in the programme, except do it a lot cheaper, please.'

The unexpected, however, happened yet again as Saddam Hussein, the President of Iraq, ordered the invasion of Kuwait. Britain and America quickly agreed to co-operate in the expulsion of the invaders. Defence policy had again been shifted from the Continental commitment to an expeditionary operation.

The Final Legacy

The SDR had all these previous reviews as a background but it also had an immediate legacy in the forces and equipment, traditions and capabilities that were currently in place. The major equipment types, in particular, could not be replaced quickly or cheaply, since such projects take in the order of ten years to reach fruition. Equipment that would be deemed surplus to requirements by SDR could be, by contrast, easily scrapped. Traditions and capabilities represented the accumulation of years of hard-won experience and had to be weighed carefully. Powerful voices could be expected to comment on the possible disbandment of long-established units and the capabilities they afforded. On the other hand, to be effective, SDR had to reach logical, rational conclusions divorced from sentiment and emotion.

There were also two particular issues from the past that were carried into the Review. The Trident weapons system provided the British nuclear deterrent and was excluded from consideration in SDR. It is arguable that, if the Trident system had not been in service with the Royal Navy, it would not have been bought as part of SDR, despite its being a powerful protection for homeland UK. The Eurofighter programme had long been in gestation and decisions as to the purchase of the British tranche of this collaborative venture with European partners needed to be taken. As a result, the first tranche of this programme did not form part of the SDR discussions. It is virtually impossible to undertake a review without untidy legacy programmes overriding the logic of the process.

Continuity

Legacy can also been seen as continuity. The past informs the present and, if existing structures, etc., have proved to be effective then change is unnecessary, unless evidence can be produced to invalidate that assumption. The view of the value of tradition held in Britain is sometimes seen as a subject for mild amusement abroad but long-standing practice incorporates the wisdom from the past of what works and what does not. It has to be conceded, however, that this process can be taken to lengths that impede change. Continuity and legacy are, then, to be treated carefully to extract the value but leave aside the dead weight of inertia. Continuity was briefly discussed when the Select Committee on Defence questioned the Secretary of State and Mr Hatfield (see Annex B to this paper).

The Current Debate

The 2009 ippr paper, 'Shared Responsibilities' suggested the following widening of the concept of defence:

> The objective of a national security policy should be to protect the UK population from the full range of risks so that people can go about their daily lives freely and with confidence under a government based on consent. (p. 9)

Later, on page 39, the paper called for a more coordinated approach to defence policy formation to accomplish this widening of the objective from 'defence' to 'security'. The implication was that government would have to approach policy formation more holistically and would have to break down the 'stovepipes' of the separate departments. So, the next defence review will have its own legacy.

Discussion

Defence reviews are usually dreaded within the MoD, (perhaps as P.G. Wodehouse metaphor described, with the deep sigh uttered by Prometheus when his vulture dropped in for lunch). Lord Robertson recalled (interview 2nd July 2009) how he had produced a 'flyer' giving details of SDR and its aims, which contained a cartoon figure exclaiming, 'Oh no! Not another defence review.' Reviews usually meant threats to current programmes and the likelihood of cuts and reductions in the budget, because historically, they had been at the behest of the Treasury.

This financial pressure caused the individual Services to fight for their share of the budget, which led to internecine battles. The problem is summed up in the title of Baylis (1989), 'British defence policy: striking the right balance'. The right balance, however, does not necessarily mean fair shares for all and the analysis can often mean that one Service suffers disproportionately, as the Royal Navy did in the Nott Review. In fact, the fair shares approach might indicate that the planners could find no better way of deciding priorities which could indicate intellectual sterility or the lack of the necessary ideas to effect a change. Long running battles, like the competing claims for the continental against the maritime strategy, tend to re-emerge in reviews because the choice between these two basic strategies has always been contentious and controversial. The exercise of air power, too, has been the cause of battles that might have led to the disbandment of the Royal Air Force in the 1920s and can reappear in the shape of the perennial arguments over aircraft carriers. Defence reviews, then, can be the cause of bitter argument.

Reviews have, traditionally, been conducted within the walls of the MoD and outside interference has been avoided by the claims for the need to protect sensitive information. The way this work had been done reflects the balance of power at the time within the Ministry. Jackson and Bramall (1992) powerfully tracked the long struggle for greater centralisation of power in the Defence Staff, at the expense of the single-Service Chiefs and their departments. A more 'purple' Ministry, it was hoped, would achieve that dispassionate analysis of the defence needs of the nation and be freed from the pleadings of land, sea and air for priority. Since the Central Staffs were peopled by uniformed officers that objectivity is difficult to achieve because the individual's career after the Central Staff tour would be back with his or her Service which might remember 'disloyalty'. The centralisation of power has, therefore, tended to confer more power on the civil service staff which provides continuity and the analytical skills for dealing with technical, military advice. In the days before the central staff, the civilian members of the single-Service departments spent most of their working lives with the navy, the army or the air force departments and were committed supporters of 'their' Service. In the case of the Royal Navy, this tradition goes back to Samuel Pepys in the 17th century. The crucial step in the centralisation of defence policy was to break that link.

The history of defence policy in Britain is one of decline in the face of a worsening national macro-economic performance and fiscal contraction. Successive governments have been reluctant to accept the concomitant erosion of Britain's position in the world. We can exert disproportionate influence because of our experience in world affairs but our shabby gentility can be cruelly exposed when real resources are required to back up our pretensions. Our previous ruling of territories overseas is often now an embarrassment, as the Falklands War showed. Our success in this and other campaigns such as the operations in Sierra Leone may show a continued skill in limited military operations but we no longer have the resources for fighting larger conflicts without allies and, thus, our capacity for an independent strategy is severely limited. Gray (1999:10) commented:

> *Like Imperial Germany, Nazi Germany, and the Soviet Union, Imperial France pursued political goals that were beyond its means. That is a failure in strategy.*

Defence, in common with many other governmental activities, develops its policies incrementally in response to changes in the environment. Small changes of direction are less risky than fundamental shifts in policy but, after a time, this drift results in a situation in which a marked change has become necessary. Maybe, external events, like the end of the Cold War, or internal changes to the available resources, perhaps following a devaluation of the currency or an economic recession, destroy the fit of defence policy with the environment. Perhaps an unforeseen event, like Suez or the Falklands, exposes weaknesses in current strategy and then a step change becomes necessary. In the latter case, a review is likely to be welcomed by the Armed Forces as a means of rectifying blatant shortcomings in equipment, organisation or training. In 2009, such a feeling is growing within the body politic and a major review cannot be long delayed. Richard Hatfield commented (20th April 2009) that the period since 1998 has been the longest without a review since the start of the twentieth century.

Britain's long involvement in military operations creates a legacy that can lead to a circular argument which goes: we have a military capability which provides options for foreign policy, so the Foreign Office takes up these options ensuring the continuation of these military capabilities. The circle is usually broken by the Treasury who can refuse to fund the demands of the Ministry of Defence but the commitments often remain and the armed forces are forced to punch above their budget. Robinson (2005) argued against capabilities-based planning and urged a return to a threat-based approach, or moving from a bottom-up to a top-down process for determining force levels and capabilities.

Summary

Defence policy has undergone considerable change over the years and yet there is much continuity in ideas and practices. Politicians tend not to understand defence and this area is often the first to suffer in times of financial stringency. The strain then is often taken at the front line. The nature of conflict, too, changes over time which requires modifications to military structure and equipment and currently defence is conceptually being widened into 'security'. These changes may well necessitate modifications to the structure of governmental departments and the roles that they perform. The relations between those formulating defence policy and the UK defence industry have not always been harmonious but the possible decline of a UK based industry would have strategic implications. The existence of military capabilities may have an effect on the processes of a strategic defence review in that the policy may seek to use them, rather than argue whether they are required at all.

6

The Structure and Conduct of the Defence Review

In this chapter the process adopted for the Strategic Defence Review (SDR) is described but the analysis of the effectiveness of the process can be found in Chapter 8.

The Strategic Defence Review of 1997/98 was unique in that it adopted an open structure that encouraged the participation of anyone who was so moved and it developed its policies from the inputs of other Departments of State and many individuals, under the overall guidance of the staff of the Ministry of Defence (MoD). This approach honoured a commitment made by the Government in its election manifesto but the incoming politicians had little idea how to implement their proposals in detail. The civil servants in the Ministry, however, had made their usual preparations for the incoming Government and had the experience of reviews under the previous Government, so they had a structure in mind. It was fortunate too that Sir Richard Mottram, who had conducted the detail of the 'Options for Change' and 'Front Line First' exercises for the previous Government, should now be the Permanent Under-Secretary in the MoD. Some overriding parameters had been set out in the Government's General Election manifesto and were not subjects for discussion in SDR:

a) strong defence;

b) security based on NATO;

c) retention of Trident;

d) multinational arms control;

e) people in defence were of overriding importance.

An important part of the preparations for the Review was bringing the politicians up to speed on the intricacies of defence and the armed forces. Mr Robertson had not been the Shadow Defence Secretary whilst in opposition and was reported to have exclaimed, 'Oh no, not defence!' on his appointment (Essenhigh interview 24 September 2009). (There may have been a slight confusion here because Lord Robertson (interview April 2009) recalled producing a pamphlet called 'Oh No! Not another Defence Review' which although brief and in cartoon form effectively captured attention, particularly in Parliament.) One side benefit for the MoD staff who were engaged in this briefing, education or indoctrination process, was that they could get to know the person with whom they were dealing and learn to work with him effectively.

The Process

The process by which the SDR was conducted was complex, as might be expected of such a large undertaking in a large bureaucratic organisation. The structure for the conduct of the Review was devised in the MoD and the work was managed by the Vice Chief of Defence Staff (VCDS) and the Second Permanent Under Secretary (2nd PUS). By the end of 1997, VCDS and 2nd PUS were holding weekly oversight meetings to review progress and to coordinate the vast amount of work being conducted throughout the Ministry. Although the Review was divided into phases, these were not watertight compartments and the work was iterative, going back over old ground when the need arose.

There was an overriding need for the process to be logical and factual, since any poor reasoning would lead to a challenge from the Treasury. The audit trail of a logically sound argument was thought to be the best defence against those searching to eliminate expenditure. The resultant policy had to be completely justified by foreign or national policy imperatives. The Review was to be based upon the needs identified by foreign policy, whilst keeping costs to a minimum. The most recent revisions of defence policy had been conducted by a special staff, closed off from the rest of the MoD, but SDR was to be in the hands of the normal staff and conducted openly. Despite the danger of conventional thinking, it was felt that the staff dealing with issues day-to-day were best equipped to provide practical answers based on experience. Inevitably, there were individuals and groups who had their own agenda but the arguments had to be open and, thus, subject to the scrutiny in the various committees that were established to monitor progress and conduct the discussions.

The diagram at Figure 6.1 appeared in the second part of the final document, the Supporting Essays, and shows how the policy was to be formed from a Policy Framework, amplified by Planning Assumptions from which the detailed work could proceed.

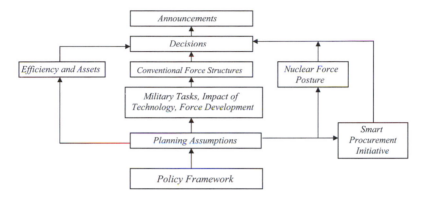

Figure 6.1   **The Stages in the Strategic Defence Review (from Essay One)**

Phase 1: Policy Framework

The first phase consisted of generating the Policy Framework which was based on foreign policy guidance provided by the Foreign and Commonwealth Office (FCO).

Sir Nigel Essenhigh recalled (interview 24 September 09) that the first document received from the Foreign Office did not properly address the policy issues and was declared to be unsatisfactory by the then Mr Kevin Tebbit, DUS Intelligence and Crisis, in the Foreign Office. The three-star Mr Tebbit personally attended a two-star-chaired meeting in the Ministry of Defence where he undertook to redraft the document himself. The resulting document formed the basis for all future work and was, thus, of crucial importance. It was recognised early in the process that the logical outcome of the 'Force for Good in the world' idea would mean a change to expeditionary warfare.

The policy baseline work was broken down into the following sub-tasks:

a)   Britain's major overseas interests and key policy assumptions arising (FCO lead);

b)   The changing strategic context and its possible further evolution (MoD lead);

c)   Developing security risks (MoD lead);

d)   Arms control considerations (FCO lead);

e)   Britain's major security interests against this background (MoD lead);

f)   Ways in which Britain's defence forces can contribute to advancement of the interests (MoD lead);

g)   Key strategic policy issues arising.

(D/01/Pol Planning 2/2/5 dated 1 May 2003)

The MoD clearly recognised the importance of the policy document and made so many additions that it became too large to be submitted to the Cabinet who, it was judged, would not read it all. Sir Richard Mottram (interview 12 June 09) said:

> It was a joint Foreign Office/MoD exercise, with a bit of help from DFID. (Department for International Development). And a huge effort was put into this, and a very large, long paper was written and each bit of the Ministry, including each of the Services, was very keen on what was written in this thing, because they saw it as having lots of hooks in it for the next phase... the paper was so long and so nuanced... it was realised that Ministers would never read it. So a much shorter paper was written, taken and signed off by the Ministers.

The Framework 'assessed the nation's interests, commitments and responsibilities and considered potential risks and challenges in the decades ahead and set out the overall role of defence in support of Britain's foreign and security policy.' (Supporting Essay One, paragraph 8) The Policy Framework document was not published on completion since the MoD felt that future work would impact upon it and releasing it would restrict opportunities to revisit the content if amendments proved to be necessary. Parliament and its Select Committee (see extracts from their final report in Chapter 7) criticised this delay in publication as what they saw as evidence of a lack of openness and the suspicion was that, if the policy document as written did not provide sufficient justification for force structures, etc., identified in Phase 2, then it would be amended. Assumptions could markedly affect the dimensions of the forces that arose from them. The Policy Framework was endorsed by Ministers as the basis for SDR, and the broad conclusions were set out and made public in speeches by the Secretary of State for Defence to the Royal United Services Institution for Defence Studies (18 September 1997) and in the debate in the House of Commons (27/28 October 1997). The final Policy framework document (Supporting Essays, Document Two) is appended at Annex A.

Phase 2: Planning Assumptions

'Planning assumptions convert policy into detailed guidance for defence planning. They cover the activities our forces need to be able to undertake, and the context in which they will undertake them' (Supporting Essay One, paragraph 11). This work translated the Policy Statement on the nation's intentions and wishes into the language of defence and armed force. It specified in broad terms the roles and tasks that were demanded as an outcome of the Policy Framework and formed the basis for further work to 'identify the specific force structures, capabilities, equipment and support required' (*ibid*). The main elements of this work were published in Essay 6 'Future Military Capabilities' which can be found at Annex A.

The logical analytical structure adopted was:

Foreign Policy → Defence Policy → Roles, Missions, Tasks → Resources

The first step in formulating the defence policy was the generation of planning assumptions which was labelled Segment 2a. This task was divided into the following sub-tasks, each of which was given to working groups to answer:

- Planning for what?

- With whom?

- Where?

- By whom – scope for cooperation with allies.

- Against whom?

- To do what?

- Based where?

- How many concurrent operations?

- Other issues:

  - Crisis Management Structures
  - Rapid Deployment Forces
  - NATO Reaction Forces
  - Reserves.

The work moved on to these other Segments:

Segment 2b   Nuclear forces

Segment 2c   Conventional Forces – Policy framework

- To revalidate the new Military Tasks against the outcome of Stage 2a with particular reference to:

  - The requirements of expeditionary warfare;
  - The requirements of our wider security role;
  - The security of the UK.

Segment 2d   Conventional Forces – Structures, capabilities and equipment

- Identify force packages for each Military Task

  - Pertaining to expeditionary operations;
  - Pertaining to the UK's wider security role;
  - Pertaining to the security of the UK.

- Establish the overall requirement for Force Elements taking account of concurrency and endurance assumptions.

- Review policy on European restructuring and key strategic industrial capabilities.

- Identify industrial and employment consequences of procurement options: any need for diversification assistance.

- Review of Public/Private Partnerships (PPP) in 'near' frontline capabilities – maximum use.

Segment 2e   Infrastructure support

Segment 2f   Procurement policy

Segment 2g   Efficiency/Assets

- Phase a: Each budget within the MoD to undertake its own management and efficiency audit, submitting a report;

- Phase b: Scrutiny and development of the reports from Phase a;

- Phase c: Conclusions, including establishment of forward efficiency targets and any organisational changes.

Within these segments, many Working Groups were formed to consider issues in detail and these are listed at Appendix 1 to this Chapter.

Resources were considered last because the process was to be policy, not resource, led. If the defence policy was derived logically from the needs of foreign policy, the Review, it was felt, could not be accused of following earlier examples by being constrained to produce a defence policy that matched a preordained budget.

The Structure of the Review

The logic of the Review having been decided, the bureaucratic structure for doing and controlling the work had to be devised, although it was a principle stated in Supporting Essay One (page 2) that 'maximum use [would be made] of existing structures – drawing on the expertise of our in-house staff, rather than setting up a separate Review Team'. The detailed work of the Review was done in a large number of Groups, each led at one-star level under the guidance of a two-star officer or official, which considered topics such as the naval requirement for frigates, the army's need for counter-insurgency forces, and the air force's fast jet and transport forces. The results of this work had then to be considered in the wider, policy framework, so committees at higher level were needed. Inevitably, the work of these committees was often referred back for further work if the results did not fit with the output from other such committees.

Figure 6.1 shows what had to be done and Figure 6.2 below shows the means within the MoD by which the work was to be carried out and monitored. The process had to be controlled, otherwise anarchy might ensue but too rigid control might inhibit the creative thinking that was being demanded. Mr Jon Day (interview 5th May 2009) sketched the high level structure used within the MoD during the Review and Sir Richard Mottram (interview 12th June 2009) added further detail. The model is shown at Figure 5.2

In practice, the structure was used flexibly and so, on several occasions, the Secretary of State himself chaired the low-level Internal Studies Group (ISG) when items of particular interest were on the agenda.

The Cabinet
|
The Secretary of State for Defence
|
Financial and Policy Management Group
|
Policy and Planning Steering Group
2–3 Star Level

Other Government
Departments   → |

Internal Studies Group
1–2 Star Level
|

Other Government   Working Groups
Departments   →

Figure 6.2   The MoD high level structure for the Review

The Working Groups

The detail of the SDR was conducted in the Working Groups, with two-star officers made responsible for them, and their work was to be monitored by an appointed three-star, Mr Richard Hatfield, as the three-star DUS (Policy) and Mr Jon Day, the one-star Director of Defence Policy, were responsible for co-ordinating and monitoring the work of these many groups. The detailed account of the structure and responsibilities of the Working Groups is contained in Appendix '1' to this Chapter. The resulting papers were reviewed by the Internal Studies Group.

The Internal Studies Group

During Phase 1, the policy baseline drafts were sent to the Internal Studies Group (ISG) for consideration several times during the process. Once a final draft had been cleared, the baseline was presented through the Policy and Planning Steering Group to the Financial and Policy Management Group (see below) for final MoD approval. The ISG was, therefore, an important reference group that identified and resolved potential opposition to particular measures. A similar process took place in the Foreign and Commonwealth Office, resulting in a joint submission after internal approval from both Departments.

This mode of operation was also adopted for reviewing the output of the Working Groups, described above. The Secretary of State insisted that at least three options should be offered to the Financial and Policy Management Group for approval. Perhaps 'straw men' options were devised by the Working Groups but at least it avoided the appearance of 'take it or leave it'.

Policy and Planning Steering Group (PPSG)

The PPSG operated at two/three-star level and considered the output of the Internal Studies Group before seeking endorsement at the next level. As the name suggests, this group exercised control of the process and filtered outputs on their way up through the system.

Financial and Policy Management Group (FPMG)

The Financial and Policy Management Group was the senior committee in the SDR and was, in composition, effectively the Defence Board. If the Internal Studies Group was the engine room of SDR, the FPMG was the bridge. Mr Day (interview 5 May 2009) referred to this as a Star Chamber and it was at this level that a broader view than that generated by the detailed Working Groups could be reached. As a result, some results from the PPSG were referred back for further work with guidance as to the changes required. The final decision rested with the Secretary of State, and it was in the FPMG that the arguments were refined to a point that a choice could be made. Lord Robertson (interview April 2009) outlined his heuristic for this process 'you listen, you decide, you explain, and then you execute.'

Initiatives could be introduced at this level, rather than coming from below, and two of them, the Royal Navy/Royal Air Force pact and the creation of the Chief of Defence Logistics post are examples. The origin and discussion of these initiatives, described in more detail below as 'Anomalies', reveals a fault line that has been described in the previous Chapter and was the tension between the Defence Staff in the centre and the single-Service Chiefs. Progressive moves to make savings or increase efficiency, depending on one's viewpoint, had led to increased concentration in the Centre, and a consequent diminution of the power of the 'baronies' of the individual Services. Joint Force Headquarters had been established under Mr Portillo for the conduct of operations and single-Service operations centres now just produced and deployed the forces where and when directed.

The Cabinet

The outcomes of the SDR had, eventually, to be considered by the Cabinet for approval and the Secretary of State and Chief of Defence Staff attended a meeting of the OPX Committee (the successor to the Overseas Policy and Defence Committee) for that purpose. The Committee was chaired by the Prime Minister, and Admiral Essenhigh was chosen to make the defence staff presentation to the Committee. It was clear to the MoD team that the Chancellor was not really interested in their arguments but wanted a reduced sum for the defence budget. The DFID Minister, Claire Short, was also critical of the proposals at this meeting. Admiral Essenhigh intervened in the Cabinet discussion (which was not really within his remit) by pointing out that the proposals were alternative, not consecutive, and using a diagram drawn up to illustrate this point. Sir Nigel Essenhigh commented (interview 24 September 2009):

> *George Robertson has had the good grace to say subsequently that that was the turning moment in the Strategic Defence Review – this intervention, because that diagram said it all.*

The Prime Minister, Mr Blair, then summed up, using notes previously prepared by the Secretary, who was an MoD man seconded to the Cabinet Office, and delivered a succinct and effective summary. (The Cabinet Office itself had formed a Defence Review Steering Group). The MoD had won the policy argument but not, as it later emerged, the financial one.

Anomalies

The civil servants who set up the structure and methods of SDR did not want to have activities which did not conform to the logical, rational process they had devised and which arose outside the ordered routine. Nonetheless, at least one did occur.

'THE SATANIC PLOT'

During the Nott Review in the 1980s relations between the staffs of the Royal Navy and the Royal Air Force became so bad that staff officers would often not talk to friends in the other Service. The arguments were bitter and the expectation in SDR was that this situation would prevail in 1997. For those in the Central Staff who did not wish for the Royal Navy aircraft carriers to be replaced, such enmity offered the possibility of dividing and ruling. A similar process could be applied to the fast jet force, it was thought, in the knowledge that the RAF would support cancellation of carriers and the Royal Navy in return would oppose increases in the fast jet force. Both of these decisions would release considerable sums of money for other purposes.

The Chiefs of the Royal Navy (Admiral Sir Jock Slater) and the Royal Air Force (Air Chief Marshal Sir Richard Johns) decided, however, that their best interests were not served by this continual antagonism between their staffs, and collaborated to produce a joint paper on the issues that were dividing them. The replacement of the Navy's aircraft carriers was supported in this paper and a proposal was made for a 'Joint Harrier Force' which combined the assets of the two Services and compensated for the withdrawal of the Sea Harrier. The Sea Harrier needed an upgraded engine because in hot climates the aircraft might take off with a full weapons load but, if they were not fired, the stores had to be jettisoned to reduce the aircraft's weight to within landing limits. The expense of this procedure would be prohibitive. Fitting an upgraded engine would be very difficult technically and, thus, expensive. An offer by the Royal Air Force to give the Royal Navy some more-modern Harriers was not taken up but the proposal to combine the aircraft and aircrew of the Harrier force was adopted.

The Strategic Defence Review (Cm 3999:5) described the agreement, thus:

> As a result of a historic proposal from the First Sea Lord and the Chief of the Air Staff the Royal Navy and the Royal Air Force will build on the success of recent operations in the Gulf and co-operate to develop a new Joint Force 2000. The RAF and the RN Harrier jets of this force will be able to operate equally effectively from aircraft carriers or land bases.

The Central Staff in the MoD had expected the usual battle between the Royal Navy and the Royal Air Force and were not best pleased with this initiative which asserted the individual Services' right to determine their own destinies, at least to a limited extent. Thus, Sir Nigel Essenhigh could describe the agreement as statesmanlike but Sir Richard Johns recalled the anger of the Second PUS, Sir Roger Jacklin, at this *lèse majesté*.

THE CHIEF OF DEFENCE LOGISTICS

During the Review, the idea of combining the logistics organisations of the three Services into one, under a Chief of Defence Logistics (CDL), had been discussed but opposed by the single-Service Chiefs. The opposition arose in part from the view that this move would be a further erosion of the power of the single-Service Chiefs and the Royal Air Force was confident that their current arrangements would not be thus improved (Sir Richard Johns interview 31 July 2009). The idea for a CDL certainly gained support at the political level, where Dr John Reid had experienced the bitter arguments between the Services in the Principal Administrative Officers committee, and the proposal was pressed by the Chief of Defence Staff. No evidence has been found that the idea came up from the Working Groups. Mr Jon Day's recollection is that the idea was a core proposal from the Defence Staff and had been discussed for some time previously. The Panel of Experts in the meeting with the Secretary of State and officials on 19 March 1998 expressed 'some concern... about the concept of a Joint Logistics Organisation: we should beware creating a huge monolith at the expense of making quick efficiency improvements by introducing further private sector involvement wherever possible' (E88 MO 9/33/2J dated 20 March 1998)

Matters came to a head when it was discovered that savings had to be made from the programme that was emerging from the Review and whose cost exceeded the budget that the Secretary of State for Defence had negotiated with the Chancellor. Now, the Chief of Defence Logistics proposal was needed for reasons of cost and was pressed by the Permanent Under-Secretary and the Chief of Defence Staff. The Single-Service Chiefs were still not convinced and Sir Richard Mottram said (interview 12 June 2009) that the then General Guthrie exercised his authority as the Chief of Defence Staff to impose the decision.

Admiral Sir Nigel Essenhigh observed (interview 24 September 2009) that the assumptions as to the cost savings from this move were 'heroic' and were never realised in practice. He said of the Chiefs of Staff's opposition:

> I like to think that they were wrong. They should have embraced it. If they had embraced it more wholeheartedly to start with, it might have actually delivered more of the benefits. What they underestimated in that was the degree of change of culture that you have to go through to get such a radical change pushed through. The trouble is, if you take two very big, absolutely focussed single-Service organisations and try to weld them into one you have got to be ruthless to do it.

Mr Jon Day's opinion (interview 5 May 2009) accorded with this view and said the setting up of the Defence Logistics Organisation was insufficiently rigorous and business-like.

FINANCE AND BUDGETING

Considerations of money were always going to be a difficulty in SDR. The logical structure demanded consideration of resources as the final act, although pains were taken by the MoD to involve the Treasury in as many of their discussions as practicable. On the other hand, the Treasury were not going to give the MoD a blank cheque, into which the final cost of the SDR process could be inserted. The Treasury would not involve themselves in the detailed analysis of the foreign policy commitment and the resulting requirement for armed forces but they knew that judgements had to be made to reach the final answer. These would be informed judgements but the process opened the possibility that the budget could be reduced if pressure were to be mounted. The 'intellectually honest' (Essenhigh 24 September 2009) process was in danger of returning to the usual pattern for Reviews of being Treasury led.

External Inputs

The Secretary of State insisted that the SDR should take inputs from anyone who wished to be involved and the net was to be cast as widely as possible. During the Review, the MoD was to consult the National Defence Industries Council, the Defence Scientific Advisory Council and the Trades Unions through the Whitley Council. The MoD also conducted seminars to brief widely on the progress of the SDR and take inputs. A Panel of Experts was also formed for a similar purpose.

Essay One, page 4, of the Supporting Essays observed:

> The Secretary of State invited anyone with an interest in or a view on defence to make a submission to the process. Over five hundred submissions were received, from MPs and Peers, local authorities, academics, industry, interest groups, journalists and members of the public. They were circulated to staff dealing with the subjects to which the submissions related. All were interesting and some had a significant impact on our work.

SEMINARS

Three sets of seminars were held during the SDR process, one in Coventry, one in London and one in the MoD. The seminars were attended by the Secretaries of State for Foreign Affairs and Defence and were open to journalists, academics, and members of the public. The first two were held in the very early stages of the Review and were intended to stir up interest in the proceedings and to encourage a wide participation.

Seminars were held on 3rd and 11th July 1997:

> At both seminars officials from the two Departments introduced emerging conclusions from the early policy work which underpins the Defence

Review. These conclusion were covered under four main headings: the
UK's Major Foreign Policy Interests; the changing Security Context;
Arms Control; and the UK's Major Security interests.

(Enclosure 7/1 of D/DefPol/16/1)

In the introduction to the first of these two seminars, the Foreign Secretary
and the Defence Secretary both stressed that SDR was the United Kingdom's
review rather than the Government's, emphasising their wish for an open and
wide ranging debate.

Details of the third seminar were contained in a press release from the
MoD:

BRITAIN'S DEFENCE: SECURING OUR FUTURE TOGETHER

... The third Strategic Defence Review seminar follows on from two
very successful joint seminars previously held with the Foreign and
Commonwealth Office. A wide cross section of defence related expertise
and opinion is being invited to take part, and it will again be open to
the media. In addition the seminar will be open to members of the public
to observe. Numbers are constrained by the space available, but as Mr
Robertson commented:

The seminars to support the Review are a unique exercise in consultation
which have proved invaluable in testing our ideas. And I am particularly
keen that the public are able to observe Government at work, making
this Review a truly open process.

As part of his continuing plans for consultation, Mr Robertson also
plans to hold a series of working lunches with senior defence observers,
including former Ministers and representatives from defence, industry
and the scientific community....

(E61 D/Def Pol/16/7/3 dated 6 October 97)

The third seminar was held in the MoD from 1000–1600 hours on 5 November
1997 and was chaired by Sir Michael Quinlan, a retired Permanent Under-
Secretary in the MoD and a respected expert on defence matters. The tickets
for the public were selected by ballot to prevent 'packing' of the audience by

single-issue organisations. The outcome of these seminars was expected to be comments at the policy level, rather than details that the staff within the MoD were much better equipped to consider.

PANEL OF EXPERTS

The press release quoted above also announced the formation of a panel of experts as part of the consultation process. It wrote:

> *Mr Robertson said:*
>
> *This government was elected on a manifesto commitment to provide strong defence for the UK in a rapidly changing world. The Strategic Defence Review is now well under way; and I want this to be a Review that the nation as whole can support. To achieve this, I am determined to ensure the maximum level of outside input into the process, and I am delighted that these sixteen busy people from such a diverse range of backgrounds have agreed to be members of the panel. Their advice will be extremely important in ensuring that the Review is firmly based on the widest possible consensus on defence policy.*
>
> *The panel of experts includes recently-retired officers and officials, representatives from industry, experts from the academic community and think-tanks, from journalism and from the wider business community. The main task of the panel will be to inject expert opinion into the Review and to act as a sounding board for its emerging conclusions.*

The members of the Panel of Experts were:

Sir Michael Alexander

Janet Bruce, Lady Balfour of Burleigh

Janet Cohen

Professor Lawrence Freedman

Air Marshal Sir Timothy Garden

Lord Gladwin of Clee

Dr James Gow

Professor Colin Gray

Simon Jenkins

Richard Lapthorne

Dr Patricia Lewis

Admiral of the Fleet Sir Julian Oswald

Trevor Phillips

Sir Michael Quinlan

John Rose

Dr Alan Rudge

Colonel Terence Taylor

Field Marshal the Lord Vincent

(Annex B to SDR Process Essay, July 1998)

The Terms of Reference for the Panel of Experts were:

- The panel is being established by the Secretary of State for Defence to provide advice to the MoD on issues relating to the SDR. Its aim is to contribute towards the maximum level of outside input to the Review and to a much wider degree of national consensus on defence policy.

- Panellists will be invited to contribute views to the Review process, in their area of expertise or more widely, and to comment on issues raised by the MoD, including the Review's emerging conclusions. They may also contribute towards a full public understanding of the Review's outcome.

- The panel will not meet regularly as a body. Panellists' views will be sought, individually or collectively, in different fora as the Review develops including by Ministers.

- Some discussions will need to be on a confidential basis. Those panellists who do not have a current security clearance will need to agree to a basic security check and to sign the Official Secrets Act.

- The panel will come into being from the date of the Secretary of State's public announcement of its composition. It will cease to exist on the day of publication of the Strategic Defence Review White Paper.

- Panellists will receive no remuneration. They will, however, be able to claim legitimate expenses.

(Annex A to D/Def/Pol 16/7 dated 15 August 1997)

A diary of activities of the Panel Experts is attached at Appendix 2 and it can be seen their involvement was largely as individuals at particular events relevant to their expertise. As such, it is difficult to evaluate the inputs from this Panel, but Sir Simon Jenkins' view (email 16 Jul 09) as one of the Panellists was:

> *The lay panel for the SDR really was of no use. I think it was intended principally as a public relations exercise.*

(On the other hand, Lord Robertson (interview April 2009) recalled that he had had some very useful conversations with the then Simon Jenkins and had found his 'Devil's Advocate' role stimulating.')

Another eminent participant in the Panel of Experts observed:

> *For what it may be worth, I regard the process of consultation which the MoD sought to under take as part of the Review as having been, so far as I observed it, serious and commendable; and if, as I mildly suspect the amount of added enlightenment that was thus obtained may have proved a little disappointing, the fault cannot lay at MoD's door.*

(Enclosure 4 DDefPol/16/7/3)

The views of the value of the Panel of Experts was, therefore, mixed but it was recognised that the legitimising effect of such consultation was valuable, even though only relatively few inputs might have actually affected the outcome of the Review.

Internal Inputs

Within the MoD there were no illusions about the reception that the news of a Defence Review would receive from the serving Armed Forces and the associated civilian staff. To them, reviews meant cuts. Essay One, page 6, recorded the efforts made to counter this cynicism:

> *A key part of the consultation process was the establishment of a liaison team to talk directly to military and civilian personnel throughout defence. The team was led by a Group Captain and included representatives from all three Services and the Civil Service. They listened personally to views expressed by individuals at all levels, who were encouraged to speak frankly, and reports were made directly to the Defence Secretary. It was impossible for the team to speak to every employee, but their visit programme provided over 7,500 staff with an opportunity to discuss the Review and make their views known. It also gave Ministers a valuable insight into many of the issues of most immediate concern to Service personnel and civilian staff.*

Submissions were encouraged from Service and civilian personnel and about a hundred such inputs were received.

Interim Outputs

The Secretary of State was determined to make the SDR an open process and so he released or authorised the release of information during the Review:

- The Secretary of State made a keynote speech at the Royal United Services Institution for Defence Studies on 18 September 1997.

- The Secretary of State addressed the Royal Institution for International Affairs, Chatham House, on 12 March 1998.

- The Secretary of State published an article in *The Independent* on 30 July 1997.

- The House of Commons conducted a two-day debate on 27/28 October 1997 (See Chapter 7) and an adjournment debate on 25 February 1998.

- The House of Lords debated the Review on 6 November 1997 (see Chapter 7).

- Regular press releases were made to the national regional and press.

- A BBC television programme was screened on 31 May 1998 (see below).

- Factsheets were provided on topics discussed in the Review. 46 are listed by the MoD, and a summary of the public seminars was posted on the internet.

- NATO and WEU Secretaries General, Defence Ministers of NATO Allies, Five Power Defence Arrangements and the Gulf Cooperation Council were all kept informed by letter and at appropriate meetings.

Clearly, considerable efforts were made to keep the stakeholders in defence policy as well informed as possible: so different from previous, closely-guarded Reviews.

The BBC Television Programme

The BBC was allowed into the MoD with their cameras to film episodes in the conduct of the SDR. Their remit was to have freedom of access but they were debarred from showing any material that had a security classification. The programme was screened on 31 May 1998.

A SYNOPSIS OF THE PROGRAMME

The programme opened with suitable military music and scenes showing troops in action but much of the following material was punctuated by leading participants giving their views. Sir Richard Mottram (Permanent Under-Secretary) observed that he was the expert on process and the Secretary of State was concerned with making decisions.

Mr Jon Day, a Director on the Policy Staff, was shown briefing the MoD staff on the conduct of SDR at the outset and he identified the essence of the review as, 'What the forces should be called upon to do and how they should do it'. Jon Day had set up the process which would employ 40 different working groups, which were to identify who would do the operations and how they would do it. The briefing told the staff that the outcome of the review was an open question, although Richard Hatfield, Deputy Under-Secretary (Policy) said that the resulting programme could look very much like the existing one. Under the Conservative governments, the number of military personnel had been cut by a third but new commitments had arisen, like peacekeeping in Bosnia. Robertson's review was committed to ensure that future defence tasks did not exceed the resources allocated.

A problem is that officials have to judge what forces will be doing in 5 to 10 years' time and a meeting of senior staff, the Internal Studies Group (ISG), was shown studying a report on how the forces might look. The assumption on the forces' role in Northern Ireland, where the unrest was still continuing, was a significant factor. Colin Balmer, Director of Finance, said that the ISG had an, informal, knockabout style, which had been encouraged. Nevertheless, the ISG adopted a hard approach because if the individuals could not sell the ideas to the Chairman, Richard Hatfield, then the argument could not be sold to the Treasury.

The scene shifted to Mr Robertson in Russia closing an agreement under which the Russian Navy and the Royal Navy would participate in joint exercises. The aim was to build bridges between the two countries' military. It had been Mr Robertson's personal idea to promote 'defence diplomacy' to reduce the risk of conflicts breaking out, and he wanted it to be a theme in SDR. His other initiative was the open approach to the study. So seminars were to be held to seek the views of journalists, academics and defence experts, submissions were to be invited from the public and an appointed Panel of Experts from outside the MoD were to act as sounding board for the developing proposals in the Review.

Scenes were then shown of a meeting briefing the Secretary of State in preparation for his appearance before the Defence Select Committee of Parliament (see the transcript of that meeting at Annex B). The Secretary of State had decided not to publish the FCO/MoD views on defence priorities, but the Defence Committee felt that, as a result, it had been left in the dark (a summary of the findings of the Defence Select Committee is in Chapter 7). The Select Committee felt that they could not contribute to Phase 2 unless they knew the details of the agreement in Phase 1. The S of S' response was that instead of presenting to Parliament a *fait accompli*, they were being involved *before* the decisions were taken.

These decisions in the SDR were guided by scenarios, which were then developed into a military view of how the forces would respond. The programme then showed a discussion of how Britain would respond to a call for assistance from Poland. The Navy proposed deploying an aircraft carrier into the Baltic but doubts were expressed about the conduct and the validity of the Operational Analysis. The results very much depend on the assumptions and the probability assessments, as Sir Richard Mottram observed during the interview on 12 June 2009.

A proposal to cut the Reserve Forces drastically and transfer the tasks to the Regular Forces was discussed at meeting chaired by Dr John Reid, Minister for the Armed Forces. If the Reserves were not to be used in formed units, but as specialist individuals, then the numbers could be reduced drastically. (Sir Nigel Essenhigh who was shown making these observations complained (interview 24 September 2009) that this was only part of his presentation which gave a distorted view of what he actually said.) Dr Reid decided that the military case for drastically reduced reserves should be overridden by social, strategic and wider defence factors.

There followed scenes from a meeting at which the Treasury officials were pressing for savings. The MoD involved the Treasury throughout the Review, rather than at the last minute, so that they could participate in the process and observe its rationality. The Treasury, however, were concerned at the relation of the MoD spend to other Government priorities. The Treasury asked for study of a range of options, but the MoD protested that they could not study *all* options and asked the Treasury to make a selection. The Treasury accepted that they could not have the costs of all options and the MoD accepted that they would look, outside the main body of work, at those selected by the Treasury.

Bernard Gray, a journalist acting for the Government as a political advisor, wanted to 'blow away some of the cobwebs of MoD culture'. He said that more options were required for the Treasury and encouraged more radical thinking.

Some of the detailed work of the Working Groups was shown:

- A proposal for an Airborne Cavalry Brigade subsuming the Parachute Regiment which would not be used for brigade-strength drops. Lord Guthrie, Chief of Defence Staff, observed that this proposal would be opposed by the 'old and bold'.

- The size and composition of the Royal Marines was debated but doubts were expressed that the options offered were proper options. The decision was taken to retain the current capabilities.

- A team was shown discussing the C-17 transport aircraft for heavy lift and proposed that six of these aircraft were required. Their work was hampered by not being allowed to discuss options with the Americans and so leasing could not be confirmed as a possible way forward.

The output of these Groups reflected the views of those at working level and it was passed to the senior Finance and Policy Management Group for their consideration and decision.

In the final stages of the programme, Dr John Reid was seen stressing the importance of people-related issues over equipment issues and this theme was to be reflected in the Cmnd 3999, *The Strategic Defence Review*. The Programmes Office of the MoD had costed 500 different options that could save money but the figures were complicated by some overlap and duplications. The programme stated that no financial limits had been set but there were skirmishes with the Treasury and the Cabinet Office over the likely final budget amount. The MoD was seeking to identify the cost-drivers to include in their final presentation but opponents needed to understand the detail and track the logic of the reasoning, rather than make arbitrary criticisms. The danger was, Richard Hatfield observed, that the Treasury would impose an arbitrary cut on the basis that 'You will find another way of doing it, won't you?' A prescient remark.

A Summary of the Process

The Government had promised in its Manifesto that it would hold a SDR which would be policy led and open to inputs from all. The first step, then, was the MoD working closely with the Foreign and Commonwealth Office to produce a paper detailing the nation's foreign policy. The experienced officials in the MoD set about structuring the process by which the Review was to be conducted and they drew heavily upon the work of Sir Richard Mottram (at the time of SDR, Permanent Secretary in the MoD) who had crafted the 'Options for Change' and 'Frontline First' exercises for the previous Government (Richard Hatfield interview 20 April 2009).

The Policy Directorate was to manage the process and the central figures would be Richard Hatfield, Colin Balmer and Jon Day, although the overall direction was in the hands of the Vice Chief of Defence Staff (Air Chief Marshal Sir John Willis (now deceased) and the Second Permanent Secretary (Sir Roger Jacklin) (Supporting Essay One, paragraph 7). The detailed work was to be conducted in Working Groups and it was unsurprising that much was done in committee, since much of the Ministry's day-to-day work relies on meetings and committees formed for particular purposes. Mr Hatfield maintained a 'story board' as a means of tracking progress and identifying any omissions and anomalies (interview 20 April 2009). This initiative was decided at a VCDS/ 2nd PUS tracking meeting on 12 December 1997:

> ... This would show the outline and developing logic of the white paper, and would be an aid to tracking progress on the different studies and identifying issues to be addressed as they arose. The aim would be to create a living document which might be used with Ministers, to show how the separate studies would fit together, and which could be updated as necessary.

> (Enclosure 62 DDefPol/16/1)

The Internal Studies Group, chaired variously by Mr Hatfield, Mr Balmer and even the Secretary of State, as the topic demanded, provided the necessary detail.

The 'openness' promised by the Government was approached by holding three seminars, which were open to the press, academics, scientists, industrialists and the public, and were conducted in Coventry and London.

A Panel of Experts was formed of notable people in the field, although its involvement was fragmented, rather than their acting as another Working Group. Doubts have been cast by a number of those interviewed for this study as to the value of the inputs made in this way, although they were not without relevance, but the Panel of Experts and the seminars added to the legitimacy of the SDR, which was important to the final acceptance by all of the validity of the conclusions reached. A further example of the unusual openness of SDR was the documentary programme made by the BBC which gave a flavour of what was going on within the walls of the main building. The viewing public were confronted with the complexity of the process and the earnest endeavours of those involved to evolve a defence strategy for the twenty-first century, although the arcane discussion on the use of carriers in the Baltic may have puzzled those with any knowledge of defence.

Detail was generated by the Working Groups whose work was controlled by the Internal Studies Group which was the engine-room of SDR. The process was not, however, entirely 'bottom up' since the overall shape of the emerging defence policy was being formed by the Financial Policy Management Group, essentially the Defence Council, which was the political, official and military interface. It was at this latter level that judgements had to be made and decisions taken because only here was a synoptic view possible. Some work, inevitably, was referred back down for reconsideration by the Working Groups and so the process was iterative until the FPMG were satisfied. Vested interests abound within the MoD and, although their claims were defensible in a theoretical sense, the leaders of the process had to consider their value within the constraints imposed by the needs of Foreign Policy and for the creation of balanced defence forces.

The political view was provided by the Secretary of State and his Ministers who were aware of the ambivalence of the public's view of defence. The personality of the Secretary of State was important and Sir Richard Mottram's view was (interview 12 June 2009) '[he] was basically a very outgoing and consultative sort of man and he had a significant influence over the *tone* of it.' Defence is, by nature, an insurance policy and the threat to those abed in the UK did not seem to be great at that time and the size of the defence budget, although much reduced, could seem to be an excessive premium to pay. Thus, reaching a consensus on defence policy was of considerable political importance, particularly in view of the pressures from other spending Departments, such as Social Security, Health, and Education, being exerted on the Chancellor, who was not a natural supporter of things military. Parliament and the House of

Commons Select Committee on Defence also represented the diversity of views within the community and their part is discussed next in Chapter 7.

In sum, the process of the Review within the MoD was logical and intellectually honest. The MoD fielded a strong team that was given coherence by the Secretary of State who himself was open, cooperative and well-liked. Great pains were taken to involve all stakeholders which yielded some useful input and contributed to the legitimacy of SDR. The smouldering bomb was hidden in the finances.

Appendix 1:
The Working Groups in Phase 2

Segment 2c – Convention Forces (1) Policy framework

Force Development

Segment 2d – Conventional Forces (2) Structures, Capabilities and Equipment

Germany

Defence Diplomacy

Army Organisation

Search and Rescue and Fishery Protection

UN Standing Forces

Caribbean Presence

Joint Rapid Deployment Force

Command and Control of Contingency Forces

Territorial, Auxiliary and Volunteer Forces Associations (TAVRAs)

Readiness

Reserve Structures

Strategic Lift

Establishment Standards

Force Structure

Operational tour lengths and tour intervals for units

Tri-service generation of aircrew

Ground-based air defence/Nuclear, Biological and Chemical (NBC)

Forward Equipment Programmes

Future Medium Surface to Air Missile/Ballistic Missile Defence

Future Carrier Based Aircraft/Future Aircraft Carrier/Future Offensive Air System

Helicopter Jointery

ICS

Pay and Allowances questions for PX

Military Manpower modelling

Return on Investment in People

Sustainability

Logistic Support to Expeditionary and Joint Operations

Logistics:

    1.   Storage and Distribution

    2.   Information Systems and Process Convergence

3.   Strategic Movement

Segment 2f: Procurement Policy

Key Defence Industrial Capabilities

Logistics:

4.   Procurement/Logistics interface

Regeneration/Reconstitution

International Procurement Issues

Industrial and Employment implications of Stage 2d options

Procurement Issues for PX

Commercial Policies and Procurement Methods

Procurement Executive – Systems Interface

Procurement processes and procedures

Technology

Segment 2g: Efficiency/Assets

Headquarters Organisation

Assets (i)

MoD Non-Departmental Public Bodies

Innovative Proposals for Industry

Assets (ii) Review of MoD Property/Estate Holdings

Agencies

Organisation of RAF Commands

Logistics (v) Fuels and Lubricants

Stockholding, including issues for PX

Total: 52 (excluding Nuclear Forces)

Appendix 2:
Panel of Experts

Diary of Activities

The following was provided by the Ministry of Defence from their file D/Def Pol/16/7. It has been edited by the author of this book to remove names of those who could not become Panel members and whose inclusion here might cause embarrassment to them.

Note: Minister (AF) = Minister for the Armed Forces

Minister (DP) = Minister for Defence Procurement

Date   Event

8/9/97   The Secretary writes to [people prominent in foreign and defence affairs], inviting them to become members of the panel

29/9/97   Secretary of State writes to [alternatives] to replace [those who were unable to accept].

8/10/97   [Another alternative] telephoned and invited to become a panel member.

10/10/97   Secretary of State writes to panel members confirming the full list of names and the date of the announcement.

13/10/97   Names of panellists announced through a press release

29/10/97   All panellists other than Lord Gladwin meet the Secretary of State,
            Minister (DP) and Minister (AF) for lunch at Admiralty House.

5/11/97   Sir Michael Quinlan chairs the third Review seminar. Professor
            Lawrence Freedman also takes part; Sir Julian Oswald observes.

10/11/97   Janet Cohen, Sir Michael Quinlan and Lord Vincent attend the S of
            S lunch with former officials/senior officers.

25/11/97   Lady Balfour attends the S of S dinner for former Ministers.

4/12/97   Lady Balfour, Janet Cohen, Lord Gladwin, Simon Jenkins and
            Trevor Phillips attend 'teach in' with D Def Pol and Bernard Gray.

8/12/97   Lord Vincent attends Min (AF) dinner for Academics/NGOs.

9/12/97   Sir Michael Alexander attends S of S lunch with industrialists.

10/12/97   Sir Timothy Garden attends Min(DP) lunch with Peers.

10/12/97   Secretary of State meeting with Sir Michael Alexander, Simon
            Jenkins, Sir Michael Quinlan, Trevor Phillips and Lord Vincent to
            discuss Public Expectations of the Review, is cancelled.

15/12/97   Minister (AF) meets with Lady Balfour, Sir Timothy Garden and
            Dr James Gow, to discuss 'How 'joint' should our Forces become?'

17/12/97   Dr Alan Rudge attends Min (DP) lunch with Scientists.

18/12/97   Minister (AF) meets with Janet Cohen, Lord Gladwin, Richard
            Lapthorne and Dr Alan Rudge, to discuss 'Efficiency – are we
            missing anything?'

22/12/97   Documents pack sent to panellists.

23/12/97   Pack of submissions sent by courier to Janet Cohen.

5/1/98   Minister (DP) meets with Professor Colin Gray, Sir Julian Oswald,
            John Rose and Col Trevor Taylor to discuss 'Is our analysis of
            current technological trends and issues correct?'.

Handwritten Notes

S of S meetings on :   defence diplomacy

                              nuclear policy

                              public expectations

8/7/98   Panel ceased to exist on SDR publication day on 8 July 1998

7

Parliament

Introduction

Although the process of the Strategic Defence Review (SDR) was in the hands of the Ministry of Defence (MoD), Parliament continued to follow closely its progress, made inputs, and criticised, according to the individual's politics and party affiliation. The House of Commons conducted a defence debate on 27 October 1997 and the House of Lords followed with theirs on 6 November 1997. The Select Committee on Defence collected evidence during 1997 and 1998, before issuing their Eighth Report on 10 September 1998 on the SDR. The Government responded with their comments on the Select Committee's Report with their own Sixth Special Report on 18 November 1998. Extracts from the proceedings of these events and the various papers as they relate to the topic of the process of SDR are given below.

House of Commons Debate – 27 October 1997

The House of Commons conducted a debate on defence policy which was the occasion for the first statement by the new Secretary of State for Defence, Mr George Robertson. In his statement, Mr Robertson stated his intentions for the Review:

> *When I launched the review at the end of May, I said that I wanted it to be open and inclusive, not like the secretive and often partial reviews of the recent past.*

> *(Hansard Column 609)*

Clearly, the declared intention was to make the review comprehensive rather than, as in the past, addressing a few issues in an attempt to save money. The Minister expressed the view that there was a consensus on defence in the British nation and, by engaging in an unprecedented amount of consultation in the review, he wanted to establish a wide base of support for its conclusions. One of the results of this consultation was that 450 contributions had been received already from interested parties and were being considered in the Review.

He affirmed Britain's continuing commitment to the European Union, NATO and the United Nations, whilst maintaining the transatlantic link which he considered vital to our defence. He went on:

> We shall not stand aside from the new threats and problems that face the international community because that is not our way. We intend to be persuaders for our values and points of view. Britain will continue to be a force for good in the world.

> (Hansard Column 610)

Whilst observing that the monolithic threat from Soviet Russia and the Warsaw Pact had disappeared, other tensions were surfacing. He instanced ethnic disputes, religious tensions, competition for scarce resources, the drugs trade, organised crime and terrorism as problems that had now to be faced.

Mr Robertson would not be drawn by questions on spending, reserve forces and medical services, since answers would prejudge the outcome of the Review in progress. He did say that the Review was tasked with finding greater efficiencies to provide cost-effective defence. He spent some time outlining the MoD's initiatives on the outlawing of anti-personnel mines with the help of the Secretary of State for International Development (Claire Short), who was to become involved in SDR.

The Minister gave a broad account of developments following the changes to Russia and Eastern Europe and looked forward to closer links with former adversaries. He commented:

Closer work with our former adversaries will make us friends and achieve a disarmament of the mind which is every bit as valuable as an international treaty. We must use the tools of preventative diplomacy and co-operation over development to help to eliminate problems before they occur. We are now looking for new ways to engage with our former adversaries, many of which will involve a positive role for our armed forces. This work I call defence diplomacy and I intend to make it a major theme coming out of the defence review.

(Hansard Column 619)

The Minister then concluded his statement which had made a number of party political points but affirmed some political inputs to SDR, namely:

a)   The review was to be open and inclusive.

b)   It was to be policy led, although financial savings would be sought through efficiency and cost-effectiveness gains.

c)   The defence forces would be used as a force for good in the world and as a tool for preventative diplomacy.

d)   The nuclear-armed Trident missile submarines were to be retained.

The Opposition's response to the Minister's statement concentrated initially on finance, but Sir George Young (North-West Hampshire) commented that the decision to exclude defence equipment from the review poses a risk that the equipment will dictate defence policy, rather than the choice of equipment being dictated by policy. He also criticised the decision to delay publishing the foreign policy baseline because Parliament would be denied the opportunity to comment before the Review moved on to its next phase. Mr Menzies Campbell (North East Fife) spoke for the Liberal Democrats and used the term 'peace support' as one of the roles that the defence forces would have to perform.

The Minister for the Armed Forces (Dr John Reid) summed up the debate which had largely concentrated on technical defence and constituency concerns and largely accepted the methods being employed in the SDR.

House of Lords Debate – 6 November 1997

The Minister of State, MoD, Lord Gilbert moved the motion for debate, 'That this House takes note of Her Majesty's Government's defence policy'. In so doing he covered the same ground as the Secretary for State for Defence had in the House of Commons in their debate, but he added the wish for a non-partisan approach to defence matters in the life of the Government. The current debate was to be part of the process of consultation which was at the heart of the SDR process.

Lord Trefgarne expressed concern that the 'iron grip' of the Chancellor would determine the final outcome of SDR, despite an earlier assurance from Lord Gilbert (2 July 1997) that he hoped Ministers would have little difficulty in persuading their Treasury colleagues. Indeed, he recalled the Chancellor of the Exchequer stating that they were diverting funds from defence into the Health Service. Furthermore, Lord Trefgarne had heard that the funding of the Bosnia operations were to come from the defence budget rather than from the central reserve, although he conceded that this provision of some £200 million per year had not yet been decided. Lord Trefgarne concluded:

> This debate is taking place today in the context of the defence review which the noble Lord described in some detail. I have to tell him that I think that the jury is still out on whether that will be an effective and satisfactory process. Some of us are rather concerned.
>
> (Hansard Column 1490)

Lord Chalfont reflected a fear that pressures within the Labour party would have an effect on the outcome of SDR:

> Much has changed, but I think it would be right and fair to express the view that this Government also have, so far, taken a welcome and robust attitude towards defence policy. I would only express the hope that that view will not be changed by the outcome of the current defence review, when it is known. As the Minister well knows, there will be pressures, both from inside his own party and from elsewhere, to modify their policy, sometimes on financial and economic grounds, but also at a more emotional level. There will be inevitable complaints on the lines that money saved from the defence budget could be more usefully

directed towards overseas aid programmes, social services, education, health and so on.

(Hansard Column 1501)

He concluded with a fear that the process of SDR could be manipulated by vested interests:

The Minister of all people will not need reminding that dangers come not only from malevolent and aggressive forces from without, but also from well-meaning but misguided friends within. I hope that the Government will be as firm in confronting them as they appear to be in their determination to confront the external threat.

In general, the contributions to the debate were more philosophical than those in the Commons' debate and the fear that the Treasury would exact cuts to the defence budget figured in several inputs.

The Select Committee on Defence

The Defence Committee was appointed under Standing Order No 152 to examine the expenditure, administration and policy of the MoD and associated bodies.

The Committee consisted of eleven members, of whom the quorum was three. The membership of the Committee on 14 July 1997 was:

Mr Bruce George (Chairman)	Mr Michael Colvin
Mr Crispin Blunt	Mr Jimmy Hood
Mr Julian Brazier TD	Mr John McWilliam
Mr Menzies Campbell CBE QC	Mrs Laura Moffatt
Mr Jamie Cann	Ms Dari Taylor
Mr Harry Cohen	

The Committee had the power:

- To send for persons, papers and records, to sit notwithstanding any adjournment of the House, to adjourn from place to place, and to report from time to time.

- To appoint specialist advisers either to supply information which is not readily available or to elucidate matters of complexity within the Committee's order of reference.

- To communicate to any other committee appointed under the same Standing Order (and to the Committee of Public Accounts, to the Deregulation Committee and to the Environmental Audit Committee) its evidence and any other documents relating to matters of common interest.

- To meet concurrently with any other such committee for the purposes of deliberating, taking evidence or considering draft reports.

Questioning Mr Robertson and Mr Hatfield

The Select Committee heard evidence on Wednesday, 30 July 1997 from the Secretary of State for Defence, Mr George Robertson, and the Deputy Under-Secretary (Policy), Mr Richard Hatfield. The minutes of that meeting are reproduced at Annex B. The record covers a good deal of 'process' comments in amongst discussion of actual defence measures, although wider topics were addressed:

- A recurrent theme of this meeting was the decision on the part of the Foreign and Commonwealth Office and the MoD not to publish the results of their joint Policy Framework before issuing the whole Defence White Paper. The MoD clearly did not want to have their work restricted in this way, whereas the Committee felt that the work of Part 2, the detailed working out of force structures etc., needed the endorsement of Parliament to be legitimate.

- The Committee were clearly nervous about the financial issues arising from the SDR and how the Treasury might impose restrictions. Mr Menzies Campbell was concerned that the previous decisions to keep Trident and buy Eurofighter would limit the flexibility and options in SDR. The Secretary of State observed that Trident, since all the capital expenditure had been made, represented a very small part of the defence budget. Mr Robertson said that it was 'unrealistic to think in terms of increased resources for defence', and also said, 'the nation has to live within its own restricted circumstances.' Mr Campbell then suggested that the consequence could be that Britain turned down a request for involvement, but Mr Robertson replied that that was the case already and Britain had declined to participate in operations in Albania.

- There was some discussion on who would 'sign off' SDR, and how the Comprehensive Spending Review would impact on the Defence budget. The Defence and Overseas Policy Committee might agree the outcome of SDR but the Comprehensive Spending Review would not agree to the budget. Mr Robertson said that the rigour of the Ministry of Defence's review would be harder than any likely from the Treasury. He dwelt on the Smart Procurement initiative and clearly expected this move to result in significant savings.

- At one point (paragraph 137, Annex B) Mr Robertson described the SDR as 'two great Departments of State working together', but he later included the Department for International Development, Trade and Industry and the Treasury as participants, probably to emphasise the comprehensiveness of SDR.

- At one stage, (paragraph 117, Annex B) Mr Blunt suggested that the outcome of SDR might necessitate changes to Britain's foreign policy but, since this question was coupled with the issue of money, it was not answered. It was, nonetheless, a potentially important issue.

- The Committee asked if our Allies were being kept informed and received a detailed account of the formal actions taken and the contacts the Secretary of State had had with American and European senior politicians.

The session gave the opportunity for the Secretary of State to emphasise the strategic, and not just defence, nature of the Review and that it was looking 20 years into the future. He was asked about the American Quadrennial Review system and he pointed out that this could introduce an instability into the policy formation process since the time horizon was effectively only four years. The Committee clearly had some reservations on the Review, particularly that the Phase 1 results were not to be published in advance.

Other Inputs to the Committee

The Select Committee took much evidence from a wide range of respondents and two examples of written submissions can be found at Annex C. These papers were made available to the SDR team in the MoD.

The first example is a paper from Oxfam, which concluded:

> *The causes of conflict are complex and multi-faceted so any attempt to design policies aimed at conflict prevention must be based on a coherent and integrated approach. One concept which is gaining ground amongst practitioners at the moment is the concept of 'conflict impact assessments' which would attempt to judge all international policies against their ability to reduce, rather than exacerbate, the risks of conflict. In its recent submission to the International Development Select Committee, Oxfam recommended that as a first step, DFID should develop a methodology for undertaking conflict impact assessments of its own programmes and projects and report its findings in its Annual Report.*
>
> *Subsequently, we have suggested that DFID should encourage other Government Departments, including DTI, MoD, MAFF and FCO to undertake conflict impact assessments on appropriate areas of their own work, and ensure that the analysis of one department can be used to help another evaluate the impact of its decisions. Similarly, we have argued that conflict impact assessments should be applied to the work of multilateral institutions, non-governmental organisations and private sector ventures in conflict-prone countries. We hope that the Committee will consider this idea in drafting its own Report.*

This input was valued by the MoD team.

The second example is from an academic working in the defence field and considered defence budget and smart procurement issues. It concluded:

> *The SDR should prove of great benefit for UK defence policy, raising many important questions in terms of proposed force structures and procurement policy. The character of the UK defence debates over the past year or so has highlighted the value of stimulating an almost bottom-up review of UK defence activities. As the SDR moves to closer involvement of the Treasury, it is to be hoped that viable resource targets can be agreed which will permit the defence sector to evolve in a stable fashion while leaving in place incentives for greater efficiency within government and in industry.*

This input drew attention to the problems of raising the defence budget in line with inflation since this would inevitably reduce its proportion of GDP. Some difficulties were identified with the proposed 'Smart Procurement' method but questions were posed rather than solutions.

The Select Committee Report

The Select Committee published its report on the SDR (its eighth) on 3 September 1998 and noted in the Introduction that it had identified that its prime task in its first session would be to shadow the government's SDR with a view to reporting to the House on its contents soon after it was published. During the period of some 14 months, the Committee called an impressive number of senior witnesses, visited a number of defence establishments, talked to defence officials in Washington and took advice from seven special advisers.

Their analysis showed that a distinction could be made between the inescapable core of UK defence policy, such as protection from direct attack, and a range of broader objectives over which the UK had some choice. They considered whether the SDR provided a robust framework for thinking about UK defence policy, prioritising objectives and setting them within the context of constraints and alternatives. They were, in effect, shadowing the process of SDR and checking its conclusions.

They identified in their report the contextual factors:

1.   Defence spending had been falling and might continue to fall in real terms and as a share of GDP.

2.   The unit procurement costs of successive generations of many types of equipment had tended to rise significantly faster than the general rate of inflation.

There might, then, be some sacrifice of commitments or capabilities which might otherwise have been deemed desirable in order to balance the contending pressures from these two factors. The Committee were looking for evidence of such possible trade-offs. Furthermore, they looked at how successful SDR had been in addressing the problem of integrating defence policy into the pursuit of the government's wider security objectives.

PROCESS

The Select Committee reviewed the statements made on the process to be employed, which has been described in Chapter 5, and went on to consider whether the goals stated there had been achieved. They noted that the original intention was that the foreign policy objectives underlying the Review were to have been published in advance of other conclusions. They drew attention to the statement given in evidence on 25 March 1998 by Mr David Mepham, co-ordinator of the British Foreign Policy Programme for Saferworld, which is an independent foreign policy think tank:

> *Saferworld would broadly endorse what was set out in the foreign policy mission statement. In terms of how it links to the defence review, I think arguably the Government have made a mistake, in terms of the process of the defence review, in not producing a White Paper on foreign policy objectives, which could then be a matter for discussion.*

> *(Question 1187)*

Mr Menzies Campbell had put the same point to the Secretary of State for Defence, Mr Robertson, on 30 July 1997 (Question 128) and had been given this reply:

That is one argument for it but against that argument are different arguments. One is that by publishing at this stage, so shortly after an Election and just before a fairly lengthy summer recess, we might be seen to be locking Parliament itself out of the process of debate even at that first stage. The other thing is that in listening to people in the process so far – and remember that this is only the second meeting of the Defence Committee, the Government has been operating for the last 12 weeks and we have listened very carefully to the views which have been expressed to us – there has been a view that forming what may be an artificial distinction between stage one and stage two, ie trying to ring-fence a policy baseline, some huge document, some massive publication, on which you would then base a second stage, was an artificial distinction because there were interrelationships between the two. Therefore the view was that we should declare a number of the broad policy objectives that we had come to at this interim stage. That is what I have chosen to do today, and there may be other opportunities during which we can do it. But to artificially constrain us into publishing something at this point would, I think, be unfair.

We conclude that the early and separate publication of a White Paper on the government's foreign policy would have improved the transparency of the review process and facilitated wider debate and wider public involvement in the process of defining our defence and security posture. *(emboldened in the original)*

(Report paragraph 54)

The Committee went on to conclude on whether the process had been successful in building a consensus within the MoD. The Secretary of State for Defence gave the opinion that never before had such a degree of consensus been achieved within the Ministry and the Committee commented that there had been 'little of the counter briefing and self-promoting or scaremongering leaking from within the individual Services that has characterised other reviews… We found little dissent from this consensus among the Service chiefs from whom we took evidence'. (Report paragraph 57). The Reserves, however, appeared less satisfied with the degree of consultation and witnesses from the TAVRAs (that is, the Territorial, Auxiliary and Volunteer Reserve Associations) appeared to believe that they had not been consulted, but presented with a *fait accompli*.

> *We conclude that, so far as building a consensus between the Services is concerned, the SDR process must be judged a success.*

> *(Report paragraph 59)*

The Committee then went on to report on the degree to which a national consensus had been achieved. They began, 'On the question of whether the SDR has, or will, achieve a national consensus about our defence posture in the nation as a whole, the evidence is necessarily more equivocal and unreliable.' (paragraph 60).

Although the Secretary of State for Defence and the Secretary of State for International Development both conveyed a positive message, some other evidence suggested a more equivocal stance by the British public. The Committee's comment was:

> *This illustrates a broad point made by many contributors to the debate around SDR that there is a diminishing sense that anything is worth fighting a war for; the money spent on defence does not seem to be money spent on an urgent and vital necessity. It is seen as discretionary.*

> *(paragraph 62)*

One problem identified by the Committee was that the submissions from the general public were largely dissenting; but that, they felt, is the nature of such self-selecting consultations, that is, the 'silent majority' issue. The process may have been open and inclusive but it did not necessarily produce a balanced set of opinions. In these circumstances, is it legitimate to place greater credence on the evidence of 'experts', when a lone voice may be the one that speaks the truth? The opinion of the Committee was non-committal:

> **The question of whether the SDR process has significantly raised the profile of the defence debate inside and outside Parliament is one criterion by which its success will be measured over the coming months and years.**

> *(paragraph 64)*

Having been unable to form a positive conclusion on the national consensus, the Committee turned its attention to considering the degree of inter-governmental cooperation engendered by the process adopted for SDR. They observed:

> *While it seems that Stage 1 of the Review was a genuinely cross-governmental exercise, it is less clear that such interdepartmental cooperation fully informed the later stages of the Review...Sir Timothy Garden noted that:*
>
> *the SDR...points out that the military capability is only one part of the security dimension and there are all sorts of other parts...it is not clear that the process has been as thorough and as all consuming for the other sections of our security needs as it has [been] for the purely military.*

> *(paragraph 66)*

> **We are not convinced that the SDR process has initiated this interdepartmental discussion on how to respond to asymmetric threats on a consistent basis.**

> *(paragraph 67)*

The Select Committee had gathered a large volume of evidence from written sources and oral statements of witnesses and some examples are included here in Annex C.

The Government Response

The Government responded to the Select Committee Report in a paper dated 18 November 1998 which welcomed the committee's report on the SDR. The Government recorded that it could not agree with all the propositions advanced but were pleased to note that the Select Committee endorsed the Review as a plan for the future and provided a sufficiently durable strategy to last until 2015. The following are some extracts from the Government's paper.

WHITE PAPER, SUPPORTING ESSAYS AND FACT SHEETS

3.   With regard to the SDR process, the Committee has sought (paragraph 55) clarification of the status of the Supporting Essays in relation to the policy commitments within the SDR as a whole and expresses doubt about the status and circulation of the SDR Factsheets. The Supporting Essays were designed to meet the Government's commitment to much greater openness but also to make the White Paper itself manageable and readable, by bringing together in a separate volume much of the supporting detail. The SDR Fact Sheets were intended primarily as an aid to internal communication of the Review's conclusions to Service personnel and MoD employees. They were therefore designed to explain what the SDR outcome would mean for particular functional areas of the MoD, although they have also been used for external presentation; copies are available, for example, on the MoD website. The White Paper, the Supporting Essays and the fact sheets were all used in the MoD's internal communications exercise. 5,259 copies were sent to units of the Armed Forces and MoD personnel as part of a co-ordinated internal communication strategy. 470 copies of the White Paper and Supporting Essays were separately distributed to the Committee, Allies and the UK Delegation in NATO. A further 4,271 copies were prepositioned centrally in the MoD for release subsequently.

(House of Commons: Defence – Sixth Special Report)

INTERDEPARTMENTAL CO-OPERATION ON SECURITY

4.   The Government agrees with the importance attached by the Committee to inter-departmental co-operation on security issues (paragraph 67). These issues, including the potential challenges posed by so-called 'asymmetric threats', are already discussed on a regular basis in a variety of cross-departmental fora. They are well established mechanisms for the assessment of threats to British interests (including in economic and other spheres) and for intra-departmental discussion and development of policies to respond to these challenges, using all the various methods (be they diplomatic, economic or military) at the Government's disposal. The Government is determined to build on interdepartmental

co-operation of the type that characterised the SDR but sees no immediate requirement for additional structures, 'mini-reviews' or reporting on defence and security issues (paragraphs 70 and 71). However, the involvement of people from outside Government in the Review process proved to be extremely successful and this is a technique we intend to use again in the future.

(ibid)

OPENNESS OF THE REVIEW

5.   The Government welcomes the recognition the Committee has given to the fact that the SDR was the most open defence review ever conducted (paragraph 74). An unprecedented amount of information has been published to encourage informed debate on all aspects of our defence policy; this is in line with the Government's wider commitment to openness. However, the Government is disappointed by other sentiments expressed by the Committee relating to the openness of the Review (paragraph 75). In those very few cases where information has been withheld, it has been done so entirely in accordance with the Government-wide Code of Practice on Access to Government Information. For example, information which falls into the category of 'Advice to Ministers' is specifically mentioned in Exemption Two of the Code. This relates to internal discussion and advice the disclosure of which would harm the frankness and candour of internal discussion. Whilst the Government will always consider requests for information with a predisposition towards providing it wherever possible, it must be able to assess arguments and to conduct its own internal debates with a degree of privacy.

(ibid)

The remainder of the Government's response to the Select Committee on Defence's Eighth Report dealt in detail with observations on the content of the SDR.

Comment

Parliament took a close interest in the proceedings of the SDR and the Select Committee on Defence collected a great deal of oral and written evidence which paralleled that being gathered within the MoD. The open approach adopted by the MoD made possible this unprecedented involvement in detail in a public forum. Even so, the Select Committee wanted the power to access proceedings that the Secretary of State deemed to fall into the category of 'Advice to Ministers' (see paragraph 5 of the MoD's response quoted previously)

The debate in the House of Commons gave the Secretary of State the opportunity to declare his approach to the defence review and he stressed the openness of its approach in contrast to previous such exercises. He introduced his thoughts on defence diplomacy, a process by which Britain's military would engage in talks with forces, particularly in countries like Russia, which had previously be seen as adversaries. The opposition expressed fears about the influence of money on the Review and the possible interventions by the Treasury. These fears were also expressed in the House of Lords and harked back to previous reviews that had been dictated by the Treasury imposing cash limits. The Government stressed that this review was foreign policy led, although they did conceded that efficiencies were to be sought wherever possible.

It is difficult to assess the impact of these activities, given that the Government had a large majority and could be reasonably confident of passing into law whatever the Review decided. In the main, the process being adopted by the MoD was welcomed, although the Opposition in both Houses wanted to have the foreign policy baseline published in advance for debate. The work of the Select Committee duplicated much of what was going on in the MoD but its task was to monitor that latter activity on behalf of Parliament and hence the electorate.

Their views on interdepartmental consultation seem to be accepted by the Government but in their further comments it indicated that it really thought that the current mechanisms were sufficient: a view contested by the then Sir Timothy Garden. The recent (2009) ippr Report, however, identified that the 'stovepipes' of the various Departments needed to be dismantled and better means found for forming an integrated view of defence and security in its contemporary form. It would seem necessary for the process of future Defence Reviews to take account of this view, although the MoD are likely to remain the controlling body.

8

Analysis and Conclusions

Introduction

Knowledge of the future is a guess: strategy is set in the future: therefore strategy is a guess. This unpromising syllogism is not wholly true since our ideas of the future are based on forecasts which can be defined as 'informed guesses'. Although we cannot know the future, experience and commonsense based on what happened in similar circumstances in the past will increase our chances of making a reasonably correct forecast. On the other hand, we cannot totally avoid the risk of being completely wrong.

The accuracy of our forecasts in defence is influenced by what other people or states will do, and we can only assume that they will act rationally; that is they will pursue their own best interests. Allison and Zelikow (1999) question the validity of the 'Rational Actor' model but, in an uncertain future maybe twenty years hence, this is probably our only reasonable assumption. Since we may not know who is the 'enemy' in the model, the Organisational Behaviour and Governmental Politics are virtually impossible to apply. Our assumptions are also influenced by our own objectives and our view of Britain's place in the world and the commitments we should assume.

In this context, one can point out a flaw in the logical sequence of Strategic Defence Review (SDR). The Policy Framework (Supporting Essay Two, see Annex A) suggested that Britain's place in the world was 'determined by our interests', which is true in part. Mr Robertson in his evidence to the Select Committee on Defence (see Annex B) stated 'that Britain will use its assets to the full' in support of its foreign policy. The economic strength of the country will determine, however, whether we can afford to protect our interests by military power should the need arise. SDR proceeded from this foreign policy base to calculate the forces required, only at the last minute to come up against the Treasury's assessment of the resources available. The Treasury view of Britain's place in the world was different from the Foreign and Commonwealth Office's perception but the SDR process was not repeated to debate the issue of Britain's place and to adjust the policy. (Mr Blunt in questions to the Secretary of State in the Select Committee on Defence (see Annex B), asked whether the outcome of the SDR could have an impact on foreign policy but the reply denied such a possibility). There was, thus, no attempt to instigate a further iteration of the process to harmonise foreign policy, fiscal policy and defence policy

Britain is a medium-sized, moderately-rich nation which possesses, like America and France, armed forces that can be projected over long distances. But are we bound to maintain that capability? For what purposes should this power be used? Chalmers (2002:206) recalled a reaction to Britain's unwillingness to intervene in the 1994 Rwanda Genocide:

> *This inaction, it was argued, resulted from a cynical unwillingness to use military force except when direct economic or strategic interests were at stake.*

Is it fair to label such unwillingness 'cynical'? The New Labour slogan, 'A Force for Good', suggested that Britain would act on moral, rather than economic or strategic, grounds. The idea seems to go back to the idea of Britain as the world's policeman and one which:

> *... is governed by a convoluted mixture of historical prejudices, humanitarian impulses, international expectations and perceptions of 'vital interest'.*

> (Sabin 1993:269)

But can Britain afford to act on moral grounds alone, where no economic or strategic interests are involved? Even if Britain could find the necessary resources, given the contending uses for the nation's wealth, would the public, that is the voters, support such a priority? Would you know the majority view until they voted you out of power?

At the outset then, the Ministry of Defence (MoD) had to contend with the very essentials of strategy: that it addresses an uncertain future, it is dependent on assumptions and there is an existing legacy from the past.

The Uncertain Future

In the 1970s when 'long range planning' was the vogue, forecasting was widely used, until the first oil crisis arrived unannounced and to the dismay of the seers. One company, Shell Oil, however, did better than most because they had eschewed forecasting in favour of scenario planning, which acknowledged that they were unlikely to be able to predict exactly what was going to happen. Instead, they imagined various stories of what might happen in the future, from the optimistic to the pessimistic, and then considered how they might, in broad terms, deal with each eventuality. Schoemaker (1992:68) described the technique:

> The basic idea is to identify existing trends and key uncertainties and combine them into a few future worlds that are internally consistent and within the realms of the possible. The purpose of these scenarios is not to cover all eventualities but to discover the boundaries of future outcomes.

The SDR process followed similar lines in that it did not consider operations against particular enemies but identified *types* of conflict that needed to be addressed. Then an assessment was made of the size of forces required (battalion, brigade, division, etc) to tackle these types of conflict. From this assessment a generic list of missions could be compiled. In this way, a start could be made towards deciding the total force levels required, although how many of these operations could be undertaken at the same time was a significant assumption.

Assumptions

The probabilities of events, such as weapons system failures, percentage serviceability of equipment, etc., are derived from data gained from tests, as is weapon lethality. Such statistics make it possible to run a computer-based game of a particular plan, which will give an indication of the likely outcome. The shortcoming of this particular approach is the dependence on the assumptions that are made. For instance, will the enemy act in the way assumed? Are the assessments made of the effectiveness of *his* weapons valid? Will the weather be as assumed? The cynic would say that, 'Give me the outcome you want and I will give you the necessary assumptions!' This may be an overstatement, but protagonists will probably make the assumptions that will not undermine their case, and then aver that gaming 'proves' their assertion. Much depends on the assumptions one makes, although it is possible, using sensitivity analysis, to identify the critical ones. There still remains the problem that, because the approach uses the Monte Carlo method, the outcome will be only probable, not certain. Run the game again and the result might be different.

Probably the crucial assumption in SDR was the coincidence of certain scales of action: that is, how many and of what sort of conflict would Britain be called upon to face at the same time? The assumption was that Britain could mount two, consecutive, medium, brigade scale operations simultaneously but if a divisional-scale operation then emerged, the medium scale would have to abandoned. These relatively modest assumptions generated, nevertheless, considerable logistic implications.

The Legacy

Seldom does the strategist start with a clean sheet of paper and SDR was no exception. Details of its legacy can be found in Chapter 5. In one respect, the legacy was helpful in that senior officials involved in SDR had already conducted somewhat similar exercises in 'Options for Change' and Front Line First', although not in the open fashion demanded by the new Secretary of State. The logical structure employed, however, was similar and proved to be a valuable template for the new challenge. Legacy as continuity was beneficial.

Another part of the legacy was the collapse of the Soviet Union and the resulting perception that the Cold War was over. The forces at that time were only sluggishly mobile but the removal of the threat to Central Europe released these forces for other policy options. The selection of the expeditionary force option could be seen as taking the opportunity to do what the nation had wanted to do for some time or, alternatively, finding a use for the Armed Forces to avoid taking another severe cut.

The United Kingdom, in contrast to Canada, maintains separate armed forces in the Royal Navy, the Army and the Royal Air Force and each is headed by its own Chief of Staff. Although warfare has to be conducted as a joint effort, the existence of any of the three Services is not justified alone by the support they give to the others. As there is a land war, so there is a naval and an air war with objectives and tasks in their own right. So, in addition to supporting the naval and land operations with defensive and offensive air power, the Royal

Air Force may well have to fight an additional war for air supremacy against the enemy. The Royal Navy, too, is concerned similarly with operations against enemy naval power. That these campaigns have not figured since the Gulf War does not mean that they can be ignored for the future. Arbitrating between the powerful cases argued by each Service has always been difficult, even though nowadays much more of the Forces' activities are joint, or in the vernacular, 'purple'.

Complex weapons systems take many years to develop and cannot be wished into existence in the face of a current threat. What is in-Service at the time of a review may not meet the demands of the new strategy and new projects take years to complete. Buying from overseas suppliers, however, may conflict with the strategic need to maintain a specified level of an indigenous defence industry and the absence of possible supply restrictions.

All of these conflicting pressures suggest the need for judgement, compromise and negotiation. The legacy meant that the reasoning in SDR could not be truly *a priori.*

'Seven S'

The Seven S model was described in Chapter 2 and is used here as analytical tool to shed light on the SDR process.

STRATEGY

The strategy adopted was based primarily on the needs of foreign policy and inherent in any organisation with self-belief is the need to preserve its existence and power. The foreign policy statement opened up that opportunity to the MoD through the adoption of the expeditionary force policy. The selected strategy satisfied the needs of the MoD and the Foreign and Commonwealth Office but brought problems with the Treasury.

STRUCTURE

The structure of the MoD had been becoming more centralised, or 'purple, and the SDR provided opportunities for increasing that trend. The establishment of the Defence Logistics Organisation was a further step in the centralising tendency and had been on the agenda of the Central Staffs for some time, so the need to save money from the programme gave a justification for its adoption. The concomitant reduction in the power of the Single-Service Chiefs was, to some, a welcome outcome. In addition to the Central/Single Service crack in the system, there is the Civil Service/Military division. The officials provide the continuity and occupy a position at the political/military interface, whereas the military provide the technical expertise and try to guard the interests of those actually called upon to fight. 'Baronies' or 'silos' of vested interest are evident in the MoD, particularly since each Service believes passionately in the value of their contribution and would not willingly see their resources reduced in comparison with the others.

SYSTEMS

The workings of the MoD are both bureaucratic and hierarchical, and the process of SDR reflected both facets. The civil servants were clearly in control of the SDR process, and were upset by the Royal Navy/Royal Air Force initiative for Joint Force Harrier which was probably seen as aberration in a well planned scheme. Ministers took the decisions, although they were unlikely to reject specialist advice, but did inject their own policy ideas, such as Defence Diplomacy.

STAFF

As seen above, the MoD staff comprised long-serving civil servants and short-term military. Although both parts were apolitical in their advice the officials were, by experience, more accustomed to working at the political interface. The officials were university trained and experienced in analysis, whilst the military were almost all staff trained in military-style analysis and in deriving solutions. There was no shortage of intellectual talent.

STYLE

Defence policy is, routinely, devised incrementally and the MoD style is, thus, conservative rather than radical. The Armed Forces have a hierarchical rank structure and aspire to rather old-fashioned virtues like loyalty and integrity. The Civil Service, too, is not given to rash moves and, too, has moral and intellectual values. Hotheads may exist, particularly in the young and junior, but the system has learned over the centuries to control their enthusiasm, not the least by refusing to promote them. The MoD style is cautious, thorough and risk averse.

SHARED VALUES

Within the MoD all share the belief in the value of defence to the nation and wish to see the continued availability of military power for use, when required, to support Britain's aims and its place in the family of nations. There is the awareness, however, that within Government this view is not shared by all and many have different priorities for the country's wealth. The MoD may see defence as protecting and enhancing the status of nation but others may view it as consuming resources that would be better spent elsewhere.

SKILLS

The Civil Service is skilled at rational analysis and has learned to manipulate 'the system' to forward their ideas. The military are trained to be expert in their field and in staff work. In the Ministry, the theory of completed staff work is adopted, which offers to superiors, not problems, but options for their solution, supported by detailed analysis. This approach was evident during SDR.

The picture that emerges of the MoD is of a bureaucracy dedicated to producing solutions to the problems arising in defending the nation and its interests. The general approach is analytical and thorough and the officials provide the continuity and control the processes of the staff. Nonetheless, talented senior military officers exercise considerable power and influence, although some of this is contained within baronies of special interest. If any Ministry were to be called upon to perform a strategic policy review, Defence is probably as well equipped, or better, than any other in Whitehall. A widening of the scope of defence to encompass the wider security issues, would need a change to the methods of interaction with other Government Departments. These OGDs were consulted during SDR but in a widened SDR the power relationships would have to be different.

The Allison and Zelikow Model

Allison and Zelikow (1999) studied the strategy formulation process during the Cuban Missile Crisis of 1962 with a view to devising models for the analysis of such events in foreign affairs. The three models that they proposed provided different ways of explaining what had happened:

- The Rational Actor Model;

- The Organisational Behaviour Model;

- The Governmental Politics Model.

Their work was introduced in Chapter 3 and is used here to analyse the SDR.

THE RATIONAL ACTOR

The Rational Actor Model for analysing events in foreign affairs attempts to explain the behaviour of governments by regarding them as an individual. Thus, events are often reported in terms such as, 'The Americans invaded Iraq', which regards the government of the country concerned as a 'black box'. This 'individual' will have aims or objectives and will study the alternatives available to achieve it. The consequences of each course of action will be evaluated and then the rational choice of maximising the utility of the country (or maximising the payoff) will be made.

This 'classical' mode of analysis is widely used and will yield a result but what is going on inside the 'black box' is not clear so understanding the reasons why a particular course of action was chosen remains uncertain. This study of SDR is essentially about what is going on within the black box so the Rational Actor Model will not yield answers. This is not to say that the actors within the black box are not acting rationally, or not seeking to maximise their payoffs.

THE ORGANISATIONAL BEHAVIOUR MODEL

Occurrences are an organisational output: thus, the details of the British intervention in Iraq were arranged by defence agencies. The triggering decision will have been made by the Government but defence agencies offered the advice and specified the alternatives. The advice itself will have been derived from organisational routines, doctrine and Standard Operating Procedures. McInnes' (1998:829) observation is redolent of this model:

> ...the range of options considered may have been limited by bureaucratic pressures, internal norms and what Robertson described as sound **military** experience... and distinguished **military** traditions. (emphasis in the original)

Thus, this model suggests, governmental action, in this case, can be understood as a result of organisational behaviour within the MoD, although it received advice from other organisations, notably the Intelligence community.

Allison and Zelikow went on to list the organising concepts of the model:

a)   *Organisational Actors.*   'The actor is not a monolithic nation or government but rather a constellation of loosely allied organizations on top of which government leaders sit'.

(op.cit page 166)

b)   *Factored Problems and Fractionated Power.*   'Surveillance of the multiple facets of foreign affairs required that problems be cut up and parceled out to various organizations'.

(ibid)

c)   *Organisational Missions.*   Each government department is given a mission to perform a particular role and 'organizations interpret mandates into their own terms…Morton Halperin thus adds the concept of organizational essence, defined as the 'view held by the dominant group in the organization of what the missions and capabilities should be'.

(op.cit. page 167) (Halperin 1974: 28)

d)   *Operational Objectives, Special Capacities and Culture.*   An organisation will have a distinctive set of beliefs about how a mission should be implemented which lead to a definition of success. The organisation will develop norms of behaviour, its own set of priorities and operational objectives and a perception of what is important.

e)   *Action as Operational Output.* Organisational activity is programmed in character and behaviour in any particular case is enacted by customary routines, often standard operating procedures.

SUMMARY

The nature of the organisation, its culture, norms and objectives, affects the strategy process in that reliance is placed upon standard operating procedures and established doctrine. 'The way we do things' has a powerful influence on the choice of strategy. Since SDR was largely conducted within the MoD, that organisation had the principal effect on the outcome but other Government Departments were similarly affected by their organisational routines and objectives. Which Department prevailed in discussions and bargaining was largely determined by the power they wielded, and the Treasury was very powerful. The MoD believed in defence, others did not necessarily share that view.

THE GOVERNMENTAL POLITICS MODEL

Allison and Zelikow (1999:255) introduced this model, thus:

> The leaders who sit atop organizations are no monolith. Rather, each individual in this group is, in his or her own right, a player in a central, competitive game. The name of the game is politics: bargaining along regular circuits among players positioned hierarchically within the government. Government behaviour can thus be understood according to a third conceptual model, not as organizational outputs but as a result of bargaining games.

The political leaders in SDR had their own objectives but the ability to achieve these aims rested on the power that they could muster. Alliances within the Government were a means of augmenting individual power and the MoD and the Foreign and Commonwealth Office collaborated in this way. Other Departments were not probably attracted to supporting this alliance since the Treasury might cut *their* budget allocation to fund any increase in the Defence budget. Defence is not usually seen as a vote-winner since it does not attract general interest from the public which, again, weakened its appeal in the fight for funds. Without detailed evidence of the political pulling and hauling during SDR further analysis along the lines of this model cannot be pursued but the final outcome was clearly the resultant of political forces acting within the Government in particular for money.

THE MODELS APPLIED

Although the SDR process was logical and rational, the Rational Actor does not yield a convincing account of the strategy formulation process. This model does not illustrate what is going on within the 'black box' of the review.

The Organisational Behaviour model does have an application to SDR in that the routines and operating procedures within the MoD were a strong influence on the strategy formulating process. The 'foreign policy – missions – force structure – resources model' is a typical military/defence approach and the doctrine used in the three Services determined the outcome, even though there was an encouragement to apply radical thinking. For instance, the amalgamation of the three Services into one joint force would not have been given sufficient support, even though there would have been some adherents within the Ministry. Such fundamental changes would have extended the already long period taken by SDR and would have been seen as disruptive and risky. Radical change is risky and is not favoured in the essentially conservative world of defence.

The Governmental Politics model again sheds light on the outcome of SDR. The logical analysis produced a defence policy that matched the demands of the foreign policy endorsed by the Government, but the necessary resources were not provided. The Treasury had evolved their view of the balance of expenditure within the Government and their process could also be seen in terms of the Organisational Behaviour model. The Secretary of State for Defence negotiated with the Chancellor of the Exchequer but could not secure the finance necessary for the programme that had emerged from SDR. The Prime Minister was involved in these discussions but did not impose his will on the Chancellor (Lord Guthrie interview). The Secretary of State for Defence's judgement was that further pressure on the Treasury risked a reduction of the budget rather than any increase and ended the argument. The budget was insufficient for the desired defence policy, even though further savings were made, and the logic of the SDR process was compromised. This logic demanded that the argument returned *ab initio* to the foreign policy statement to seek a reduction in tasks in order to save money but this course of action was not adopted. The political bargaining determined the defence policy and left a gap in the finances that would affect the MoD for years to come. In the terms of this model, SDR though not a failure, produced a sub-optimal output.

Resource-Based View

The Resource-Based View theory has it that competitive advantage stems from the resources of intellect, knowledge and capital assets that the organisation holds. The strategy to be adopted needs to capitalise on these advantages and to exploit them imaginatively. To be effective, the organisation's resources need to be rare and imperfectly imitable. These assets can be tangible or intangible, but must be exploited fully by the strategy.

The British armed forces have rare skills which can only be imperfectly imitated but their tangible resources have been in decline since the Second World War. In size, they are much smaller than the large powers, such as the United States, Russia and China, to the extent that the operations that can be conducted without allies are limited. The skills that they have, though valuable, are insufficient to give Britain, standing alone, competitive advantage over many states in the world. The link with the United States is valuable to Britain for the status it confers and to the Americans for our influence with the rest of Europe. The relationship, however, has involved us more deeply in some conflicts than we would otherwise wish to be, and has cost us lives and treasure. Since we have no defined threat to our homeland, military operations can be undertaken as a matter of choice, rather than necessity, and in support of our foreign policy goals which have been defined as:

- *Security* of the United Kingdom and Overseas Territories and peace for our people by promoting international stability, fostering our defence alliances and promoting arms control;

- *Prosperity*, promoting trade and jobs at home, and combating poverty and promoting sustained development overseas;

- *Quality of Life*, protecting the world's environment and countering the menace of drugs, terrorism and crime;

- *Mutual Respect*, spreading the values of human rights, civil liberties and democracy which we demand for ourselves.

(Supporting Essay Two: The Policy Framework)

The task in SDR was to convert those goals into a defence policy by defining the way that the armed forces could support diplomacy by 'politics with additional means' as Clausewitz has it. The rare and valuable resources that are our armed forces have to be applied where and when they could achieve the above goals. Unfortunately, this complex and difficult exercise was not determined by such arguments but by limiting the funds available. There was insufficient debate within Government to relate the solution to our perception of Britain's place in the world and our share in contributing to world peace and stability. The Resource Based View does not seem to yield any insight into the strategy formulation in SDR.

Bower-Burgelman

The Bower-Burgelman model saw strategy being developed by the activities at working level, filtered in the middle management and endorsed or rejected at the top levels of the firm. At this level of detail, the model seems to fit SDR very well. Bower found that projects were developed at the working level and could only succeed if they were given impetus by middle management, which imposed a political development, since the success of that division of the company (or 'silo') depended on the success of such projects. In the MoD, projects arise from Operational Requirements and the successful realisation of the project, be it new ship, new tank, new aircraft, is important to the standing of the particular 'silo' in which it is located. There was opposition within the MoD at the time of SDR to the replacement of the Royal Navy's carriers and the agreement between the Royal Navy and the Royal Air Force frustrated attempts to have the project cancelled.

Although there are elements of fit between Bower-Burgelman and SDR, their model does not expect that there will be strategy inputs from the top. In their model, the top management were decision makers who adjudicated between different proposals, largely on the basis of the degree of sponsorship or impetus injected at middle levels. In SDR, the Secretary of State himself added 'Defence Diplomacy' to the mission if the armed forces, which made a strategic addition to the outcome of the Review. Strategy formulation is much messier than the purists would wish.

Ephemeral Factors

Following on the thought that strategy formulation in practice is not the structured, ordered process that it is designed to be, elements of chaos are ever present. The chaos is not of the order suggested by Cohen, March and Olsen (1972) but is present in the myriad of chance events that occur during the process. If the SDR were to be repeated using an identical structure to that of 1997/98, the process would still be different because the *dramatis personae* are different and thus have different personalities and characters. Chance elements can affect the outcome of discussion of a topic: absence of a player through sickness; the effectiveness of the replacement; family problems of a participant; if the meeting is after a good lunch; etc, etc. There may have been a chance meeting in the corridor or in the street which exchanged relevant information. Perhaps an important telephone conversation that would have affected the outcome could not be made. The Strategy as Practice School of strategy formulation seeks to capture these minutiae which may or not be relevant to the strategy that emerges. The intervention by Admiral Essenhigh in the Cabinet Meeting, when he was only supposed to give the presentation and nothing else, is an example of these fleeting actions that prove to be significant. There must have been many such during SDR and they remain unrecorded.

An Evaluation Model

Rumelt (1980:187) suggested the following model as a means of evaluating a strategy:

> *Of the many tests that could justifiably be applied to a business strategy, most will fit within one of these broad criteria:*
>
> - *Consistency. The strategy must not present mutually inconsistent goals and policies.*
> - *Consonance. The strategy must represent an adaptive response to the external environment and to the critical changes occurring within it.*
> - *Advantage. The strategy must provide for the creation and/or maintenance of a competitive advantage in the selected area of activity.*
> - *Feasibility. The strategy must neither overtax available resources nor create unsolvable subproblems.*
>
> *A strategy that fails to meet one or more of these criteria is strongly suspect.*

In terms of this evaluation, the SDR arguably passes the first three tests but fails the fourth. The Foreign and Commonwealth Office stated the objectives of Britain's foreign policy and this paper was signed off by the Cabinet. The MoD conducted a logical and thorough conversion of these objectives into a defence policy and a force structure. The Treasury made an evaluation of the allocation of funds to defence in the context of a government-wide spending review. The defence policy, however, did not match the Treasury's allocation of funds so the strategy was flawed, but not in its logic. The solution to the problem seems to demand that a return should have been made to the foreign policy objectives for a reduction in commitments, although these were only broadly stated. Perhaps the MoD's interpretation of these objectives needed to be revisited but this was done several times, and in different ways, when the financial problem became evident. The Treasury were approached to provide more funds but declined. The Government wished to have the defence policy but did not want to pay for it: a situation well known to the MoD. In the end, the MoD undertook measures, some of which were already under discussion within the Ministry, to save the required sum of £2 billion but the assumptions of how much these would save were over-optimistic and the budget carried the consequences into future years, some say to the present.

Summary

The Labour Party had included in its manifesto an intention to conduct a defence review on taking office, so the civil servants within the MoD had begun to think about what had to be done. The SDR of 1997/98 followed on from a long line of similar reviews but was markedly different in its approach in that the new Secretary of State had decreed that it was to be open and inclusive, taking evidence from whomsoever cared to become involved. In previous reviews, the work had been kept firmly within the walls of the MoD and had been driven by the need, imposed by the Treasury, to save on resources. In 1997, when the New Labour government assumed power there was a determined attempt to base this review on the needs of Britain's foreign policy for the use of armed force, if necessary, and the nation's perception of its place in the modern world. It was not so ingenuous, however, as to assume that whatever budget emerged from this process would be funded by the Treasury without question. Indeed, a realistic assumption was that no increase in the defence budget would be allowed and any desired increase in capability would have to be funded from efficiency savings.

Although the incoming government had a clear idea of the policy bases for the review, they had no structure or process for its conduct in mind. The civil servants in the Ministry, however, had been aware of the incoming government's intentions and had prudently made outline plans based on their experience of reviews. The process was designed to be logical and rational, starting with what needed to be done by defence, followed by what assumptions should guide the planning and then, through a process of thorough consultation, working out what was needed and how these forces should be organised. This process had to be controlled to avoid false logic and irrational behaviour and inputs were expected to be made from the Groups studying the detail up through the filtering process to ultimate sanction by the Secretary of State. It was to be expected that the upper echelons would refer some work back down to the Groups for further consideration but inputs like Joint Force 2000 from the Royal Navy and the Royal Air Force cut across the way that the process was designed to operate.

This latter initiative was not, however, irrational, in that the two Services involved had produced a plan that sought to prevent any alternative that might have damaged their interests. The problem for the Review was, however, that the adoption of this plan would add a further constraint to the work of the appropriate Groups which were expecting to take regard only for the Policy Framework and the Planning Assumptions. The openness of the Review cut across the logic of the process. The same comment can be made of the proposal for a Chief of Defence Logistics, which arose from a need for efficiency, but which also resonated with a desire in some quarters for a further centralisation in the defence structure as a whole.

In terms of the theories of strategy formulation, the operations of the Working Groups and the Policy and Planning Steering Groups were designed to be rational and logical: the Rational Actor model of Allison and Zelikov. This work, however, was under the control of groups who were operating more under the alternative models: Organisational Behaviour and Governmental Politics. Thus, it would seem that these three models can be operating at the same time during the strategy formulation process as the situation is perceived to demand, and are not choices for the process as a whole.

A Final Evaluation

It is now possible to draw conclusions from the evidence adduced.

- The SDR was to be foreign policy led, and Phase 1 saw the production of the Policy Framework document. The foreign policy was a continuation of traditional objectives, with the addition of an intention for Britain to be a force for good in the world. No indication was given of a reduction in commitments, nor that Britain was to accept a lowering of her position in the world. When the resulting defence policy was not allocated the required resources, there was no reconsideration of the Policy Framework.

- The process was to be open and considerable effort was expended to give everyone an opportunity to make a contribution. Notable moves were the open seminars, the formation of the Panel of Experts and the event in the Queen Elizabeth Hall. The quality of the inputs were mixed but if few made radical inputs, the commonplace observations could be seen to be supportive of the policies of the MoD and thus the consensus that was sought by the Government.

- The process needed to be logical and rational and a number of committees were set up to provide the necessary checks and balances. Within the MoD, the process worked well and the details generated at working level were skilfully brought together to produce a coherent policy. The sequence 'Foreign Policy → Defence Policy → Roles, Missions, Tasks → Resources' is logical and intellectually sound.

- The process saw detailed information and analysis at working level progressively evaluated and compiled into the wider, synoptic picture. Some work was referred back for a reappraisal, so the whole process was iterative. The resulting options were evaluated by the Finance and Policy Management Group and the final choice made. The final package was agreed by the Cabinet.

- Despite the success of the process within the MoD, the resources that were shown to be necessary were not provided by the Treasury. Nevertheless, the MoD continued with the policy that their analysis had produced and undertook measures designed to bring the budget back into balance. The amount of savings to be generated by these moves was overestimated and the MoD had money problems for years afterwards.

- The budget shortfall was to be exacerbated by the Treasury decision to raise the annual defence budget by a percentage determined by the Retail Price Index, whereas the inflation in MoD's prices was nearer 6 per cent. The defence budget reached a low of 2.1 per cent in 2002 as a result. Thus, not only was the MoD denied the budget that their Review had determined, based on foreign policy requirements, but the inadequate budget was further reduced year-on-year.

- The conclusion that can be drawn from the above is that the Government, as a whole, lacked a coherent, coordinated, synoptic view of Britain's place in the world and the resources required to maintain their current aspirations. As Lindblom's theory has it, government strategy is formed by muddling through and, perhaps, one can add, having aspirations above their income. But then, we have always wanted the penny and the bun.

A Future Review?

When the next defence Review is carried out, a choice of process will need to be made between:

- An open review like SDR where anyone who wants to can make a comment. It can be argued that this process is democratic, but not altogether efficient. The open structure raises costs and adds time,

- A closed review conducted by the experts in the Departments concerned. The core of SDR was in the hands of experts and comments from outside do not seem to have changed the outcome fundamentally: but they might have.

If the need is for consensus, the choice would point to the first solution. Lack of popular support for defence policy is likely to lead to problems but there is no reason to believe that solution b. would necessarily generate divisive solutions.

A review that determines what the Government would like to do in the world is almost certainly going to cost more than the Treasury are willing to fund. A compromise solution is likely to result in the Armed Forces taking the strain and to continue to have to punch above their weight.

Either approach needs an input of options from the working level that is aware of the practical issues and the judgement of experienced decision-makers at the top. The decisions taken will be far reaching and could well be proved wrong by unexpected future events. On the other hand, hedging by building in added flexibility is expensive. All that can be done is to rely on logical argument and experience. A future defence review will face different problems to SDR but there is much in the processes of the SDR that could be copied to advantage.

Annex A:
Supporting Essays

Supporting Essay 2 – The Policy Framework

1.   The Government's General Election Manifesto said that we would conduct a Strategic Defence Review 'to reassess our essential security interests and defence needs [and] consider how the roles, missions and capabilities of the armed forces should be adjusted to meet the new strategic realities'. The starting point was the Government's Manifesto commitments to a strong defence against post-Cold War security challenges, security based on NATO, retention of the nuclear deterrent combined with progress on arms control and a strong defence industry.

2.   The Review has been foreign policy-led and the first stage, conducted jointly by the Foreign and Commonwealth Office and the MoD, provided the policy framework for subsequent work. Its analysis and conclusions, which are summarised in this essay, were tested against a range of outside views, including in two open seminars.

3.   For most of the post-war period, British defence planning was dominated by countering the massive threat from the Soviet Union and by withdrawal from our overseas empire. There was little foreign policy choice in how we organised our security. That situation has been transformed by the end of the Cold War and by the new co-operative partnership with Russia and the countries of Central and Eastern Europe. The disappearance of the Soviet threat was a result, in part, of the effective system for collective defence in Europe which we played a key role in creating and maintaining.

NATO has evolved to become a positive force for stability and confidence for the whole of Europe. We now have a real opportunity to devise a security posture which will support and underpin all Britain's interests overseas, in a world where democracy and liberal economic systems continue to spread.

4.   The new challenges we face will call for the combined application of all the tools at our disposal – diplomatic, economic, trade, developmental, as well as the Armed Forces. In the changed world there is a new and growing role for preventive diplomacy which brings all these tools to bear to avert conflict before military intervention is required. However, this essay necessarily focuses on the defence dimension.

5.   Britain's place in the world is determined by our interests as a nation and as a leading member of the international community. The two are inextricably linked because our national interests have a vital international dimension.

6.   Britain is a major European state and a leading member of the European Union (EU). Our economic and political future is as part of Europe. British security is indivisible from that of our European Partners and allies. We therefore have a fundamental interest in the security of the continent as a whole and in the effectiveness of NATO as a collective political and military instrument to underpin these interests.

7.   Our economy is founded on international trade. Exports form a higher proportion of Gross Domestic Product than for the US, Japan, Germany or France. We invest more of our income abroad than any major economy. Our closest economic partners are the EU and the US but our investment in the developing world amounts to the combined total of France, Germany and Italy. Foreign investment into the UK also provides nearly 20 per cent of manufacturing jobs.

8.   British economic interests and our history give us other international responsibilities. Over ten million British citizens live and work overseas. We have 13 Overseas Territories spread around the world. We are members of many important international organisations

and have developed close ties of friendship with countries in every continent. And as an open society, we are easily affected by global trends and other external influences.

9.   A nation's foreign policy must reflect its values. Britain stands for a strong world community, where differences are resolved fairly and peacefully. Our national security and prosperity thus depend on promoting international stability, freedom and economic development. As a Permanent Member of the United Nations Security Council, Britain is both willing and able to play a leading role internationally. We have a responsibility to contribute to a strong world community. But we cannot achieve all our aims alone. Instead, we need to work through strong partnerships and alliances, particularly the EU and NATO. We also attach immense importance to the international community as a whole working together through the UN and other international organisations.

10.   This is summed up in the four broad foreign policy goals outlined by the Foreign and Commonwealth Secretary on 12 May 1997:

    – *Security* of the United Kingdom and Overseas Territories and peace for our people by promoting international stability, fostering our defence alliances and promoting arms control;
    – *Prosperity*, promoting trade and jobs at home, and combating poverty and promoting sustained development overseas;
    – *Quality of Life*, protecting the world's environment and countering the menace of drugs, terrorism and crime;
    – *Mutual Respect*, spreading the values of human rights, civil liberties and democracy which we demand for ourselves.

Security Priorities

SUPPORT TO THE CIVIL POWER

11.   Support to the Civil Power in Northern Ireland has been a major task for our Armed Forces. The future of Northern Ireland must be determined with the consent of the people. The Government is committed to reconciliation between the two traditions and to a political settlement which commands the support of both. The

Good Friday Peace Process marks a new beginning in this respect and the Government is committed to its success. We must, however, maintain the ability to combat terrorism of all kinds throughout the United Kingdom.

EUROPE

12.   Changes over the last decade have radically improved the security context for Britain, but the collapse of Yugoslavia has shown how instability in Europe can escalate into conflict and spill over borders. Collective security based on NATO, the transatlantic link and the continuing development of a more effective European Security and Defence Identity in NATO through the WEU, continue to offer the best guarantee of deterring and insuring against new security risks in Europe.

13.   Our military and political contribution to NATO is effective and highly valued. But because of increased operational commitments in support of foreign policy, many areas of our forces are now suffering from severe overstretch, with unprecedented short gaps between operational tours. This has effects on morale and retention.

14.   It will remain in our interests to continue to play a leading role in the Alliance. If our contribution fell significantly, NATO's ability to undertake crisis management and peace support effectively would be reduced, our ability to influence NATO in ways which reinforce our security would decline and we would send a dangerous message to the US about Europe's willingness to share the burden of security in our region.

OVERSEAS TERRITORIES

15.   There are at present no immediate threats to these Territories. We must, however, be able to react to any emerging security problem and where necessary to assist the civil authorities.

OUTSIDE EUROPE

16.   Outside Europe, our interests are most directly affected by events in the Gulf and the Mediterranean and we have bilateral understandings with some Gulf States which carry the strong expectation of military support. Risks in these areas are likely to grow rather than decline. This does not, of course, mean that we need to recreate a standing or permanent military capability 'east of Suez'. Elsewhere the risks to our interests are either small or we have more choice over the level of our response, which would be generally in combination with others.

17.   At the same time our planning needs to address new challenges: weapons proliferation, ethnic tensions, population pressures, environmental degradation, drugs, terrorism, crime and the failure of state structures.

18.   These new sources of conflict can have a direct impact on Britain. Over 90 per cent of the heroin on our streets comes from Afghanistan, where the civil war makes it impossible to tackle the problem at its source. In an increasingly interdependent world, such global problems can undermine the international structures on which we and others depend. With Britain's unusually wide overseas interests and assets, including the ten million British citizens overseas, we are particularly vulnerable. The number of such conflicts is increasing. In its first four decades the UN authorised 18 peace-keeping missions; in the past decade it has authorised a further 25.

19.   We cannot turn our backs on the human suffering and economic and social damage which such crises cause. Our international stature and influence gives us a responsibility as well as an interest in responding to them. Our forces have a range of skills and capabilities which are particularly valuable in this context. Our primary means of tackling these problems are through preventive diplomacy and economic, social and developmental co-operation. However, military force, including its deterrent effect, can have a significant role to play when other forms of conflict prevention have failed.

20.   There will be more calls on our Armed Forces to become involved
       in averting, managing or countering these new security challenges,
       with other NATO Allies or other countries. We should retain the
       ability to become involved when it is in our interest to do so and it
       will be important to have clear objectives, criteria for success and
       an exit strategy.

21.   Our forces also make an important, often unsung, contribution to the
       spread of stability and democratic values through training and other
       forms of military assistance (now known as Defence Diplomacy);
       and through anti-drug operations at home and abroad.

22.   Our own interests require the international community as a
       whole to support and contribute to actions to ensure international
       security. To encourage others to help shoulder the burden, Britain
       should take on a share reflecting the spread of our interests and our
       political leadership role, particularly in the UN Security Council.

The Defence Contribution

23.   The Armed Forces make a major contribution to Britain's objectives
       in this rapidly changing world. They must not only be able to carry
       out the range of daily tasks which may arise from current priorities,
       but also be sufficiently robust and flexible to cope with the longer
       term, when circumstances and priorities may change.

24.   Our analysis has shown that to do this, our force structures and
       military capabilities need to be based on:

       –   ensuring European and therefore British security through a
           commensurate national contribution to the maintenance of
           NATO as a politically and militarily effective Alliance. This will
           include maintenance of nuclear deterrent forces (while pressing
           for multilateral negotiations towards mutual, balanced and
           verifiable reductions in nuclear weapons), the ability to make
           an appropriate contribution to a regional conflict in Europe
           involving our NATO obligations and retaining a framework on
           which it would be possible to rebuild over the longer term to
           meet a greater threat should one begin to emerge;

- keeping the ability to respond, in combination with others, to threats to our important interests, in the Gulf and the Mediterranean. At the upper end of risks this could require capabilities which are similar in scale and nature to those which would be required for a regional conflict involving NATO;
- providing support to the civil power in meeting internal security challenges in the United Kingdom and the Overseas Territories;
- responding to lesser risks to British interests beyond these areas and to other direct calls on our forces, including any threats to Overseas Territories, assistance to British nationals overseas and support to wider British interests at home and abroad. In responding to many of these risks, we would normally seek to operate in conjunction with others. We would not expect to maintain additional forces or capabilities specifically for these purposes;
- supporting the Government's wider international responsibilities, including as a Permanent Member of the UN Security Council, particularly in relation to the maintenance of peace, international order and stability, humanitarian principles and democratic rights. Tasks of this sort are likely to be increasingly important and may require a demanding range and scale of capabilities, although participation in individual operations will generally be a matter of choice;
- helping to counter the risks from emerging global security problems such as proliferation, terrorism and international crime.

25.   Our vital stake in European security, our very important interests in the surrounding regions and our wider international responsibilities could each involve us in modern, high intensity conventional warfare. In all these cases, we could face opponents equipped with powerful modern equipment because of the increasing proliferation of weapons and technology. We therefore need forces which are flexible, highly capable, mobile and responsive. Recent experience has also shown us that our wider international responsibilities are now involving us in peace support operations where success depends on deterring or out-matching indigenous forces. This again requires forces trained and equipped for demanding conventional forces.

26.   The work summarised in this essay formed the basis for the subsequent stages of the Strategic Defence Review. We believe that all measures in the Review package are consistent with its conclusions.

Essay 6 – Future Military Capabilities

The following paragraphs are a copy of the 'Process' section of Essay 6

3.   To translate the Review's policy framework into a detailed basis for determining Britain's defence needs, a comprehensive set of planning assumptions was developed. This methodology has been used before but it was refined and expanded considerably during the Review.

4.   The first step was to define the Missions which the Armed Forces must be able to undertake in support of foreign and security policy and develop them into specific Military Tasks. The Missions are set out below, and both they and the Military Tasks are described in detail in Annex A.

THE MISSIONS OF THE ARMED FORCES

a)   PEACETIME SECURITY

b)   SECURITY OF THE OVERSEAS TERRITORIES

c)   DEFENCE DIPLOMACY

d)   SUPPORT TO WIDER BRITISH INTERESTS

e)   PEACE SUPPORT AND HUMANITARIAN OPERATIONS

f)   REGIONAL CONFLICT OUTSIDE THE NATO AREA

g)   REGIONAL CONFLICT INSIDE THE NATO AREA

h)   STRATEGIC ATTACK ON NATO

The most important changes from previous analyses are the establishment of Defence Diplomacy as a distinct Mission and the decision that we should no longer maintain forces solely to meet a strategic attack on NATO – an attack on the scale of the Cold War is no longer within the capacity of any conceivable opponent and to recreate such a capacity would take many years.

5.   The next step was to consider the level of forces or scales of effort over and above those required for day-to-day commitments (such as Northern Ireland) that we should be able to contribute to different Missions, taking account of Britain's national interests, operational requirements, Allies' capabilities and our military strengths. These assumptions were also influenced by recent experience of operations, such as the Gulf conflict, Bosnia and many smaller deployments, and an assessment of future trends and requirements. It should be emphasised that the scales of effort are planning tools; they do not prejudge the size of an actual commitment in particular contingencies, which could be larger or smaller depending on the circumstance. The principal scales are:

– small scale: a deployment of battalion size or equivalent. Examples include the ARMILLA patrol in the Gulf, the British contribution to United Nations Forces in Cyprus (UNFICYP), and the Royal Air Force operations enforcing the no-fly zones over northern and southern Iraq;

– medium scale: deployments of brigade size or equivalent for war fighting or other operations. An example would be our contributions to the NATO-led Intervention Force (IFOR) in Bosnia;

– large scale: deployments of division size or equivalent. The nearest recent example would be our contribution to the Gulf War coalition, although on that occasion the British division deployed with only two of its three brigades. Large scale is the maximum size of force we would plan to be able to contribute to peace enforcement operations or to regional conflicts outside the NATO area;

– very large scale and full scale: these comprise all the forces we plan to make available to NATO to meet significant aggression against an ally. This is the most serious single scenario that we might now face. The two scales differ primarily in the warning time available for response to the emergence of a major threat.

In both cases, we would assess that the warning time we would have available would be many months or even years.

6.   We then considered the levels of readiness applicable to different sorts of operation: that is, the notice period within which units must be ready to deploy from their bases or other designated areas. The readiness required of a unit helps to determine the level of manning, equipment, training and logistic sustainability, and also whether it must be Regular or could be Reserve. The aim was to match readiness to political and military requirements, including warning times where applicable. Account has also been taken of campaign sequencing, or the phases in which operations are likely to unfold, recognising that the readiness of forces should be graduated in accordance with the likely timescales for their employment.

7.   Another important factor is the likely duration of operations and the potential need to sustain a deployment for an indefinite period – *endurance*. The possibility that some operations will be enduring (as in Cyprus where we have taken part in UNFICYP since 1964, and more recently in Bosnia) has a significant impact on total force structure, as there must be sufficient units to be able to provide for the rotation of those actually deployed at any one time.

8.   We also considered the number of operations, of a given scale of effort and duration, that we should be able to conduct at any time – *concurrency*. This is crucial to determining the size and shape of force structure needed in the modern world, where military planning is no longer dominated by a single worst-case scenario. Our conclusion was that not to be able to conduct two medium scale operations at the same time would be an unacceptable constraint on our ability to discharge Britain's commitments and responsibilities. It would, for example, oblige us to withdraw from an enduring commitment such as Bosnia in order to respond to a second crisis.

9.   Finally, emerging trends in the relative importance of different aspects of defence capability were identified, to guide force development and ensure that our forces have the capabilities they will need, rather than those we needed in the past.

10.   Taking all these planning assumptions together, we concluded
       that the size and shape of our forces are dictated by two main
       requirements:

       – the challenge of conducting two concurrent medium scale
          operations – one a relatively short warfighting deployment,
          the other an enduring non-warfighting operation. For many
          elements of our force structure this is the most demanding
          scenario;
       – a full scale operation, which is the most demanding scenario for
          the remainder of the force structure.

11.   On the basis of the planning assumptions, we carried out an
       exhaustive analysis of the force elements required for each Military
       Task and thus of the numbers of each force element required overall.
       The methodology used, the attribution of force elements to Military
       Tasks and the consequent numbers of each force element are set out
       in more detail at Annex A. The remainder of this essay sets out the
       main results of this process in terms of future force structure.

Annex B:
Examination of Witnesses by the Select Committee on Defence 20 July 1997[1]

Witnesses: Rt Hon George Robertson ,MP and Mr Richard Hatfield

Chairman

101. Thank you, Secretary of State, for coming at very short notice. You look as though you have aged at least 15 years in the last ten weeks, but that is par for the course! Many congratulations on occupying that role. We hope that appearances by the Secretary of State are not merely annual events, we hope we can speak to you quite frequently and you would wish to come to speak to us quite frequently. We are taking evidence today on the mechanics of the Strategic Defence Review. You have sub-titled that, 'Securing Our Future Together', whether the acronym SOFT displays any subliminal message to the country or to ourselves, only time can tell! Maybe this session ought to be Hearing About the Review of Defence, which has the alternative acronym HARD. Since I have been on this Committee it seems constantly to be examining reviews, and before I was on the Committee there was a protracted review under Roy Mason and before him endless reviews. So this is the latest in a very, very long line of reviews and I hope when the review is published and acted upon at least there will be a degree of stability, as far as is possible.

---

1   http://www.parliament.the-stationery-office.co.uk/pa/cm199798/cmselect/cmdfence

I think we all owe our Armed Forces to have a degree of stability so they know where they are going to be in any future requirements laid down by our country as a whole. I wonder whether, Secretary of State, you would like to make introductory remarks? As we have all read the *Independent* today perhaps you need not be quite as long as otherwise you would have been, but for those who have not read it or listened to the radio, perhaps you will be about five minutes or so and then let warfare commence?

(*Mr Robertson*)   Surely not! Can I thank you for your congratulations on my appointment which was a matter of great personal pleasure and pride to me. Can I, in turn, congratulate you on becoming Chairman of one of the House's principal Select Committees and I wish you luck with your job as well, and I do hope that given the important relationship between the Ministry of Defence and Parliament that the Select Committee is going to play a big part in helping us to get over our message about how important defence is to this country and how we can improve it as we go along. I have to admit or confess that I had not noticed the acronym of the title of our review was SOFT. The very opposite of what we intended to be. I also have to say that I set out an early objective when I was appointed to try and abolish acronyms in the Ministry of Defence – I swiftly realised it was going to be easier to solve Bosnia! I have decided that both of them should at least get the maximum effort, and I am gradually making an impression on the acronyms despite that fact that you have managed to find one I had not even noticed. Can I just say a few words so that in many ways I might correct some of the things which have been said, not in my own article in one newspaper – I do not know if everyone reads that newspaper, the *Independent* – but what other people were ascribing to me in other forms of the media. This Strategic Defence Review, which we promised before the Election and was a critical part of our Manifesto, is designed to give the Armed Forces of this country a coherent and stable planning basis in the radically changing international and strategic context of the post-Cold War world. I think that is a commendable objective which I am sure the Committee would agree with. We have emphasised from the outset that it will be a policy led review. Our first aim has therefore been to identify in broad terms our national defence, security and wider foreign policy objectives to provide a baseline for more detailed work on the contribution to that policy which can be made by our Armed Forces. I want to tell the Committee about the emerging themes so far this morning and I would welcome your comments and views and indeed your questions. There is going to be an opportunity for the House itself to consider these matters on the first two days when we come back in October in a debate which was announced by the Leader of the House last week. Because defence planning and especially the development and production of equipment is a long-term business, our analysis has looked forward over the next 20 years. We have assessed Britain's major overseas and other security interests and how they might be affected by the changing international context during that time, and in particular how potential risks and challenges to our interests may change. Against that background and the Government's foreign policy objectives, we have sought to identify likely security and defence planning priorities. That work has been carried out jointly, and I think this is a unique aspect of this review, by the Ministry of Defence and the Foreign and Commonwealth Office but we have also tested our ideas and emerging conclusions against views received through the wide consultation exercise we have set up. The two public seminars which the Foreign Secretary and I conducted in London and Coventry, which were attended by Members of the House as well as others, have been particularly valuable. I am very grateful for all the contributions we have received – about 450 so far – and which we are continuing to receive as well. As you know, Chairman, at the end of the Cold War there has been a radical change to European security and that has led to substantial cuts in our defence spending and in the size of our Armed Forces. But the post Cold War world continues to change rapidly. Some of the changes are welcome, of course, for example the spread of democracy through Eastern Europe and Central Europe, the signing especially of the NATO/Russian Founding Act. Other events have brought new security risks and problems however and new commitments for our Armed Forces. Indeed it has been said for the last 50 years we had Armed Forces which were largely designed not for fighting but for preventing fighting, in the eight years since the Berlin Wall collapsed we have Armed Forces which are designed for use and have indeed been used to the maximum during that. It is one of the great ironies of that period. In Europe today we can see how instability can too easily escalate into major conflict in Europe. We have wide international interests as well. Indeed our Election Manifesto made it clear when it said that Britain cannot be strong at home if it is weak abroad, a new Labour Government will use its assets to the full to restore Britain's pride and influence as a leading force for good in the world. That is what we promised and indeed that is one of the clear missions of this Government. We have a major stake in world peace and stability because international trade matters to this country and we have to ensure the safety of 10 million British citizens who live and work overseas. We also have responsibilities as a leading nation in the international community and there is plenty of evidence that we must be prepared to respond to new challenges from sources such as weapons proliferation, the drugs trade, terrorism, ethnic and population pressures and the break up of some existing states, as well as the sort of aggression we saw from Iraq in 1990. So from this picture of the world, a broad sense of long-term defence planning priorities emerges. We must deploy, in that wider international context, all of the tools of international diplomacy, whether economic, trade, diplomatic, developmental – as well as military in order to ensure our national objectives are achieved. But European security remains fundamental providing effective collective defence for nearly 50 years. Its role is still vital in consolidating European security, including through building constructive new relationships with Russia, Eastern Europe, Ukraine and its ability to undertake peace support missions has been very important as have been proved in Bosnia. We must, therefore, make a contribution which helps to sustain NATO both as a politically and militarily effective Alliance. The Armed Forces of this country must also be able to provide support as necessary to the civil power. I think that many people forget that in meeting internal security challenges in the UK and its Dependent Territories. For the moment the capabilities to counter Northern Ireland-related terrorism remains a key requirement of our Armed Forces. Beyond Europe, risks to our interests are likely to be greatest in the Gulf and the Near East. We must be ready to respond appropriately, in combination with others, to support stability in that region. We must of course fulfil our responsibilities to our Dependent Territories. Elsewhere, the risks to our specific national interests may well be smaller. We would expect to meet such risks – for example, assistance to our nationals overseas and support for wider British interests at home and abroad – from forces maintained primarily to meet other objectives. I underline that point as one of the critical early conclusions we have come to. And, of course, we have to contribute to our wider international responsibilities, especially as a Permanent Member of the Security Council of the UN. Many of our missions will involve more than one of these objectives. In Bosnia we are acting in support of both European security and as part of the wider international community. The professionalism of our Armed Forces and their range of skills and capabilities means that we can contribute to meeting these newer security risks in many ways, often in support of diplomatic and other instruments for conflict prevention. But they must also be sufficiently robust and flexible to adapt should circumstances and priorities change. Recent experience has emphasised that successful intervention in peace support missions depends on outmatching local forces and requires powerful forces trained and equipped for conventional warfare. Mr Chairman, the remainder of the Strategic Defence Review will look in detail at the roles, missions and capabilities required. That will include issues such as the readiness, deployability and sustainability needed for different types of operations; the extent to which we might have to mount operations concurrently; and the capabilities likely to be provided by allies and partners. At the same time we shall be looking at how best to procure those capabilities while making the most efficient use of defence resources and assets. At a time in this country, when domestic programmes are under so much pressure, value for money for the taxpayer is absolutely critical to any view you take about defence. The British people want strong defence for this country but they do not want defence at any price and we must justify every pound that is spent in the defence budget. The review is going to include a ruthless examination of how value for money for defence procurement, one of the most important aspects of the review, can be improved. I am therefore launching a major initiative to try to eliminate the kind of cost overruns and delays that have characterised some equipment projects in the past and which this Select Committee has drawn attention to. Both industry and the Department have a part to play in this, by spreading best practice and learning from experience at home and abroad. If all our procurement projects performed as well as the best, we would secure real benefits for the Armed Forces and for the taxpayer. So we are looking for 'smart procurement'. Just as we have smart missiles and smart weapons, we need to have smart procurement as well. That means building up our range of modern procurement techniques, some of which are already being applied in the Ministry of Defence and others which are being developed elsewhere. We will vigorously examine reform of procurement practice in other countries and in the private sector to ensure that we are, in our Ministry, at the forefront of international best practice. Public/Private Partnerships will be a major component of that new approach. I shall also be looking for ways for to achieve a strong, capable and competitive British defence industry, which is a strategic part of our industrial base as well as the defence effort. The longer term sense of direction stemming from the Strategic Defence Review will provide industry with the vision it needs to guide investment and realise projects of the highest quality to meet the needs of our Armed Forces. The Government is also committed to maintaining competition as a route to achieve value-for-money and we will be looking to see that the benefits of constructive competition are also obtained at the level of our second and third tier suppliers. For example, we will be looking to increase the speed with which new technologies can be brought into operational service; to improve the mechanisms for collaboration with our allies; to drive the cost of defence equipment; and to ensure that the most appropriate support arrangements are considered and set in place throughout the life of a project. Smart procurement also means looking for simplified procurement procedures, for more reliance on commercial technologies and processes, for co-operative use of information technology with industry and for the adoption of 'lean manufacturing' in which some

British companies already have a world lead. I want to make better use of the Ministry of Defence's resources by introducing more cost-effective weapons, procured more quickly, and that I believe is an objective you would heartily agree with. The Procurement Executive of the Ministry of Defence is already changing and will change more because smart procurement means improved performance through better use of people's skills, better accounting for our resources, better IT support and better procurement processes. It will use the nine-element British Quality Foundation's Business Excellence Model, a standard much used in industry, to assess the degree of improvement. The search for smart procurement – and I underline that this is a very strong message I bring to the Committee today and I know it strikes a chord with much of the Committee's work in the past – will be a consultative process. The Armed Forces, Ministry of Defence staff and industry will be given every opportunity to contribute ideas to this initiative and I have already been talking to industry leaders through the National Defence Industries Committee which will be arranging a seminar itself in the autumn. I welcome more ideas about how procurement can be smarter, cheaper and faster. So, Mr Chairman, the message I bring to this Committee from the new Government is that the nation's defence matters to the people of this country and to the Government. We stand for strong, sensible and cost-effective defence of the nation and we believe that is in tune with what the people want.

102. That is not a modest agenda, Secretary of State, and you would be a very smart Secretary of State if you can achieve a fiftieth of that and we will watch your progress with enormous interest. Could I ask one or two questions to start on timing, because it will be very helpful to us in unfolding our programme to know when we are going to be fully activated upon receipt of the eventual publication of this document or these documents? Can you give us some indication, and I would not expect precision at this stage, as to what month you expect the outcome of the review to be announced? Will it be announced while the House is sitting, will it be a statement on the floor of the House? So basically the date and method of announcement.

(Mr Robertson) We have already said that the report will be finalised at the turn of the year. That is one of these great British expressions—

103. That is why I asked the question!

(Mr Robertson)   It can mean January or February next year, hopefully. It may take slightly longer than that. What we are concerned about is making sure we deal with this matter thoroughly enough to make sure it is robust for the future. That is making exactly the point you made, we have seen too many hasty reviews in the past. I think people want clarity and some vision for the longer term. But at the same time it has to be quick enough not to create instability and uncertainty especially in the Armed Forces where it can have a dramatic impact on morale. So we extended our timetable of six months to slightly longer than that because the summer intervenes in the process. I think that saying 'the turn of the year' is a reasonable objective because, critically, it allows Parliament to have the opportunity, both the House of Commons in the debate which has already been announced and the House of Lords at a time of its choosing, to be part and parcel of that. It would be expected that in the early part of next year we would conclude the review with the publication of a White Paper and with a parliamentary debate. But in the meantime I am underlining to the wider community that we want maximum participation because we want to achieve the widest possible consensus of the outcome so it can help the country and especially the Armed Forces.

104.   Do you envisage a period of further consultation on the outcome of your recommendations? I know it seems rather ironic, having gone through a protracted process of consultation, to then say there will be further consultation but we will want to evaluate your evaluation.

(Mr Robertson)   I would anticipate a period of evaluation after the Government has arrived at its conclusions. I do not think you ever stop talking about a subject like defence because the challenges, and the methods of dealing with the challenges themselves, can change. We would hope to be able to get through most of the work which would be involved in coming to a conclusion by then but we would expect Parliament and this Select Committee and many others to comment on what we do and we will listen very carefully to what is said.

105.   Does it mean that decisions which ought to be taken will be put on hold? How are you going to overcome the problem of making decisions which have to be made as opposed to making decisions which can only be made after the outcome of the review?

(Mr Robertson)   Decisions which have to be made will be made and we have already said that but some of the longer term decisions which may have start points or decision times during the period of the Strategic Defence Review will have to be looked at in that context. A case-by-case basis is clearly the only way on which we can proceed. There are some decisions, like decisions on the Eurofighter jet, which in many ways were predicated by views expressed before the Election. That is why it has become one of the ring-fenced issues here because the decision had to be taken by the incoming Government in order to try and persuade our allies to move with some speed on that project. But other decisions will be dealt with as they come. I should have said at the very beginning and I apologise –

106.   I am sorry, I should have asked you to introduce your colleague.

(Mr Robertson)   I have with me Richard Hatfield, whose acronym is DUS(P), Deputy Under-Secretary (Policy) who I am trying to rename Director of Policy in the Ministry of Defence. He has appeared before this Select Committee on many occasions before.

107.   Please do not name him Director of Policy (Europe) because that would be deeply embarrassing!

(Mr Robertson)   Only for those obsessed with acronyms, Chairman!

108.   Are you considering a timescale for this review? The British tend to see six weeks as a protracted period within which policies are conceived, are you thinking of five years, ten years, 15 years? After all, the Treasury said that for ten or twelve years there would be no war and that was a pretty disastrous timescale in 1929. I must say your review is most appropriate because now defence expenditure coincides with what it was in 1933, which was slightly higher than it is today, so for those of us historically orientated there are some appalling parallels in prospect. Are you thinking of a lengthy stage within which you will be implementing policies and could this, as the French do it, be almost a quinquennial rolling programme?

(Mr Robertson)   The problem with suggesting you did it on a quinquennial basis is that you build a new instability into the process. What we have to do is try and get the basic line of policy in existence, around that no doubt capabilities and attitudes will change. We are trying to look 20 years ahead and that involves

a whole series of guesses, but a lot of procurement decisions have to be taken on that basis. Some of the equipment that is being used now is 20 years old, maybe even 30 years old, so you have to make some educated guesses about the future. I think the American example (I am not so certain about the French one) of a quadrennial defence review is not necessarily ideal. We are looking carefully at American experience but their process has produced a sort of on-going running instability in the American Armed Forces which, on reflection, they might like to avoid. So we will try and learn some lessons from them and others before coming to a conclusion on that.

Chairman: I would like my colleague, Crispin Blunt, to ask a few questions on the policy baseline.

Mr Blunt

109. Secretary of State, you have said the Strategic Defence Review is foreign policy-led and this first stage will re-assess Britain's security and defence needs in the changing international environment. You told us the work was expected to be completed in the summer, I think in reply to a Parliamentary Question. Is the policy baseline work now complete?

(Mr Robertson)   We have reached some broad conclusions and some main policy themes are becoming clear, indeed, I have outlined them to the Committee today. But the discussions inside and outside Government are on-going and we are going, of course, to listen to many more contributions before arriving at the final conclusion. We do not see there being a fixed line between stages one and two because both of them can and should go on simultaneously. I think the broad conclusions I have outlined give a clear indication of where we will have to slot in the next part of the exercise.

110. Within the Department there is obviously an enormous amount of work going on now based on the policy baseline you have given, so we can assume therefore that the work that your civil servants and military are undertaking has a clear framework, a written framework from which to operate?

(Mr Hatfield)   The Secretary of State this morning has laid out the main themes which came out of the first stage of the work on policy, and that will now be used throughout the Department, as you suggest, to guide the more detailed

work into roles, missions and tasks, both for the immediate future and the long-term. So that is the linkage, if you like. We have now got the broad policy guidance and we take it forward in detailed work in the way that you suggest.

111. So the people working to you have no more detailed policy baseline to work from than that which the Secretary of State has given to us this morning in his statement?

(Mr Hatfield) What they will be doing is turning that into detailed questions about what it means for the Armed Forces. Those are the policy objectives set out in broad terms. We will then go back and look at what that means in detailed requirements for the Armed Forces and of course that will come back to ministers with a series of options to look at and how that relates to the broad objectives they set out. So there is no rigid divide between the two processes but we have broad guidance which allows us to move forward into this detailed work.

112. Secretary of State, you said in reply to a Parliamentary Question of about a month ago you would consider whether anything would be published in advance of the completion of the report, i.e. the policy baselines, and then you replied to Sir George Young the day before yesterday saying that the first stages of the Strategic Defence Review will not be published separately. Why not?

(Mr Robertson)   We said we would consider whether there might be a case for publishing some document that established the baseline but the conclusions we arrived at (and indeed it was a view which was expressed to us in a number of individual contributions as well as at the seminars) was that this was not something which could be easily separated out into a policy document followed by an assessment of capabilities and requirements; that the two processes were actually part of the same process. So having reached some broad conclusions, the decision was taken that we could go on with that work whilst making it clear roughly what these broad conclusions had been. As it happens, conveniently on the day before Parliament adjourns for the summer recess, I can do that to Parliament through the Defence Select Committee.

113. In terms of the debate that Parliament is going to have when we return in October, we will in effect be debating the statement you have made today in the Committee, in effect the broad outline of what is going to be driving the whole structure of our defence forces in the future?

(Mr Robertson)   Yes I think Parliament, since I am a part of Parliament, would take exception to the idea that, before Parliament had an opportunity to debate the broad policy objectives of the country, they were being faced with some document from the Government and were only part of the second part of the process. That was one of the reasons why we thought publishing something prematurely was not desirable and perhaps slightly improper, given that Parliament was going to have its own opportunity for feeding into that process. I think that is a valuable if not essential part of the way in which we want to do business.

114.   Forgive me, but having listened to your introductory statement a lot of it sounded extremely familiar and is almost really a continuity of policy over the last four or five years. You talked about our major defence interests, you talked about the emerging democracies in Eastern Europe, you talked about our stake in peace and stability because of our trading patterns and our 10 million British citizens overseas. All of that was immensely familiar. How does the analysis, the policy baseline analysis, you have now produced, and which your civil servants and military are working on, differ from the previous Government's analysis particularly perhaps as laid out in the 1993 White Paper which produced the three defence roles and a force structure which flowed from that?

(Mr Robertson)   I am not surprised it was familiar, it was largely in our Election manifesto. It is actually a salutary experience, even three months after the Election, to go back and see what it was that was promised. We made it clear that we intended to build not just strong conventional defence for this country, not just to maintain the independent deterrent, as basic building blocks, but that we were going to re-energise the processes that were involved in that. Maintaining the independent deterrent would go side by side with a new energy and a new drive for disarmament negotiations which are going on in the world. We do not see it simply as a fixture, we see our national deterrent as being part of the process which will eventually eliminate weapons of mass destruction. A more active diplomatic policy, preventative policy, is also part of that. So, yes, there will be elements of continuity. I do not dispute that, because a much more robust attitude for Britain using its influence for good, than perhaps you did from the previous administration which I know you served in a completely different capacity.

115. I am delighted to hear the sentiments you are expressing, they
      are music to my ears. You talk about continuity and similarity,
      perhaps you could reflect on what differences there are between the
      statement you have made to us and the sort of policy framework
      you understood you had inherited.

(*Mr Robertson*)   The last administration – and I do not want to be confrontational
because we have tried to build a reasonable amount of consensus on that and
after the Election there has been a desire not to pick off targets from the past,
but occasionally politicians lapse into being politicians so I do not completely
apologise for it – left its Armed Forces over-stretched and with a wide range
of commitments after some of the deepest cuts that have ever been seen in the
defence of this nation. They left it without any clear sense of priorities and
objectives that they were designed to fulfil as part of the overseas policy of this
country. So it is introducing a degree of vision and coherence and stability that
will mark this administration out, I hope, from the previous administration.
We are also establishing a variety of benchmarks – an energy in international
negotiations on disarmament, our initiatives on anti-personnel landmines, the
willingness to look at defence sales in a more ethical context than previously.
All of those are different aspects of policies which I think will be quite clear to
the people, not just in the course of this Strategic Defence Review but over the
next five years as well.

116. What format do you expect the policy baseline to take, the
      development of policy now? Will it be along the lines of the three
      defence roles? There was almost an allusion to that in your opening
      statement, of troops who were dedicated to Defence Role One and
      then being available for Defence Role, in the old terms, Three. Are
      we going to see a familiar format to your work?

(*Mr Hatfield*)   I think actually there will be quite a lot of familiarity in the
analytical tools we use, partly because that is just what they are and they can
be used to express all sorts of objectives. I think the actual Defence Roles will
be a casualty here because they had effectively just been replaced, even before
the Election, by a shift over several years to expressing a rather more flexible
range of mission types. So you will see some similarity in the analysis and
that will indeed help you, when we come to the end, to compare themes the
Secretary of State described this morning into implications for specific types of
mission in the short term, and there may be different implications in the long
term because one of the major aspects of the work is to look at 20 years hence
as well as the next five years.

(Mr Robertson)   One of the things that has come out of the discussion so far in
the seminars has been the break-down of this whole approach to high intensity
versus low intensity warfare, which used to dominate the debate. 'Do you go
for a high intensity warfare capability or is it low or soft?' I think there is now
a broad consensus that those distinctions simply do not exist. That you cannot
establish peace or maintain peace in the likes of Bosnia Herzegovina unless
you have some of the tools of what used to be known as high intensity warfare.
We are trying to break away in this review from some of the pre-ordained
structural views which used to be taken and I think that that will be a healthy
way of opening the debate to the public.

117. I think I would personally welcome a statement about the need to
have Armed Forces which have a capability to out-match the local
forces against which they might be deployed. I think everyone
would welcome that. Given your remarks about over-stretch and
everything else, is it possible that the review will result in foreign
policy changes or an analysis of what our defence commitments are
which may impose new demands on the Ministry of Defence and
more resources to follow?

(Mr Robertson)   I think it would be unrealistic to think in terms of increased
resources for defence. The last Government made some pretty dramatic
changes to the defence budget and I think in the present strategic climate there
is no prospect of added resources being made available for defence. What we
see as our objective is making the resources that are there work better in terms
of the objectives that are established for the country.

118. Is it possible that you could, following the foreign policy element
of this review, find yourself burdened with having to meet more
commitments?

(Mr Robertson)   I think that is unlikely, frankly, because we have a fairly good
idea, and you have a fairly good idea, of what the commitments are that we
have at this time. I think any country has to tailor its commitments, broadly
speaking, to the resources which are available to it. We gave a commitment
in the Election that we should adhere to the spending targets of the previous
administration for the next two years. The nation has to live within its own
restrictive circumstances and defence will have to do the best it can. I believe
the points I made in relation to the changing attitude to procurement are
designed to make sure that we actually get better value for a very substantial
budget we have.

119. So you are hoping to find, through efficiency savings in the procurement budget, room to address the problems of over-stretch and making sure we can continue to deploy our Armed Forces to do the job they are deployed to do?

(Mr Robertson) The question of overstretch relates both to resources and commitment that is what we are looking at in the Review and to go beyond that would be to pre-empt the outcome of the Review.

120. But you, in a sense, have pre-empted it by saying there is no question of more resources. If we are to deal with overstretch in the Army, given the number of commitments they are undertaking and you have decided to continue to have that level of commitment, in a sense you are saying something else has to give because of the ceiling you have put on resources beyond years one and two?

(Mr Robertson) It was not a ceiling under the last administration, it was actually a serious reduction of 23 per cent in real terms in the last five years and there was still an attempt to keep the capabilities going. We are very well aware, inheriting the situation we have, of the problems of overstretch and the knock-on effects that can have on morale and on recruitment. That is why we are looking with such care at the existing commitments which are there and the way in which the country itself has to look at the inescapable commitments that we have – which everyone will agree are inescapable, and those other areas which are, for any country, optional and where choices have to be made.

Mr Campbell

121. Thank you Secretary of State, you have confirmed something I have believed for a long time and certainly through the General Election campaign, that it is unrealistic, is it not, to expect any more money to be spent on the defence budget in the foreseeable future unless there were to be presented to this country a much more acute threat of some kind than is presently directed against it?

(Mr Robertson) Even if it is at the risk of damaging Mr Campbell's reputation, I cannot help but totally agree with him!

122.   The consequence of that may well be that if we were asked to take up some additional obligations, like for example an extended commitment to the United Nations, we might have to turn that down because we did not have the resources to meet that additional obligation?

(Mr Robertson)   There are hard choices for any country just now. Indeed, there are people with very considerable obligations who, on grounds of overstretch or over-commitment, are having to say no. The last administration just before the Election made the decision, perhaps on grounds of cost maybe on grounds of overstretch, not to involve themselves in the coalition which went into Albania. We have to make choices, this country will have to make choices and the Government itself will have to make choices. But we still want to be a force for good in the world, to quote the Manifesto. I think that is a commendable objective. But to do it within resources which the taxpayer is willing to give.

123.   Do I understand that so far as you are able to say this morning, one policy conclusion has been reached and will be adhered to, namely that we will retain the capacity for high-intensity warfare?

(Mr Robertson) We have to keep a broad balance of capabilities in order that the country can do what the people of this country want us to do. There is a proper balance in that. Inside your high intensity capability and your low intensity or soft capability are a wide range of options which other countries have sampled. What we have rejected is what the British people over the years have rejected, that is the idea of minimal defence.

124.   If you take peace-keeping in Bosnia, for example, if ten years ago you had said to the people in this Committee, or indeed in the wider defence community in Britain, 'We shall be keeping the peace as part of forces using 155 mm howitzers and Apache helicopters' one or two eyebrows would have been raised at that idea.

(Mr Robertson)   I think you are right. In many ways you have to see it on the ground to realise just how important some of that equipment has been in establishing the psychological atmosphere that has protected a degree of peace. My colleague, the Foreign Secretary, is in Banja Luka this morning and I know that he will be shown what I was shown when I went there in May, the big guns, the AS90s, the tanks, which are there and have given a clear signal to that community that the international community has run out of patience; and given the civil authorities, the civil process, an opportunity for getting to work without the slaughter which was going on before they came.

125.   There are some givens, are there not, in this discussion of policy? First of all, there is the Eurofighter to which reference has already been made and I believe the Government is committed to the same numbers as its predecessor, keeping the possibility perhaps of an additional 80. There is a four-boat Trident fleet, as I understand it, although there may be discussions about the number of warheads and the number of missiles. There is also the likelihood, as we have agreed, that there is not going to be any more money for defence unless some more acute threat presents itself. These are three fairly important posts, if you like, in the discussion. By fixing on posts of that kind, then of course inevitably you reduce the scope for variation in other areas, do you agree?

(Mr Robertson)   Yes, you can to a certain extent, but the budget for Euro-fighter is not going to be paid next year. It will be spread over a long number of years to come. The component of our £22 billion annual budget, as it is this year, to procurement in total is £9 billion, so there is a spread across that field. That means although there is public perception that we are going to buy 232 Euro-fighters, I want to mitigate that by saying it is spread over a long number of years, as the planes come into service. Similarly with the four submarines that make up the Trident fleet, we are committed to maintaining Trident as well as ...

126.   Four submarines?

(Mr Robertson)   Yes, indeed, we have always made that clear. The vast majority of that expenditure is behind. The estimate now, the very, very firm estimate, is that the nuclear deterrent operating costs will be some £200 million a year, a mere 1 per cent of the defence budget. So in terms of establishing your staging posts some of these staging posts are actually at the moment quite small and therefore there are still choices which can be made within a fairly large budget.

127.   Yes, but once you commit yourself to the production phase of Eurofighter, unless something very substantial happens, you are committed to buying 232 or 238 – I cannot remember –

(Mr Robertson)   232 to be absolutely correct.

128.   Can I just press you on this question of the fact, as you said in
the answer to Sir George Young on Monday, that the first stage
of the Defence Strategic Review will not be published separately?
Those of us who have any interest in the subject will know the
classic definition is to establish your foreign policy objectives,
decide what defence resources are necessary to meet these and
then find the money to pay for them. As I understand it, you and
your Government have been at great pains to say that this is not a
defence review, it is a strategic review, so we can work out, rather
as you say in this article, Britain's place in the world and Britain's
responsibilities in the world. How are we and those with an interest
in this matter going to contribute effectively to the second part of
the analysis, namely the defence capabilities which are necessary,
unless we have a clear understanding of what the Government's
foreign policy objectives are going to be? Therefore, is that not a
compelling argument for the Government to publish, if you like by
way of an interim report, those conclusions which it has reached
in relation to foreign policy before we get on to discuss what the
defence capabilities will require to be to meet those objectives?

(Mr Robertson)   That is one argument for it but against that argument are
different arguments. One is that by publishing at this stage, so shortly after an
Election and just before a fairly lengthy summer recess, we might be seen to be
locking Parliament itself out of the process of debate even at that first stage. The
other thing is that in listening to people in the process so far – and remember
that this is only the second meeting of the Defence Committee, the Government
has been operating for the last 12 weeks and we have listened very carefully
to the views which have been expressed to us – there has been a view that
forming what may be an artificial distinction between stage one and stage two,
i.e. trying to ring-fence a policy baseline, some huge document, some massive
publication, on which you would then base the second stage, was an artificial
distinction because there were interrelationships between the two. Therefore
the view was that we would declare a number of the broad policy objectives
that we had come to at this interim stage. That is what I have chosen to do
today and there may be other opportunities during which we can do it. But to
artificially constrain us into publishing something at this point would, I think,
be unfair.

129. Does that mean, Secretary of State, that we are not going to hear any more from you, perhaps in a slightly different form but any more from you in substance, than is contained in this article in the *Independent* today, before we have the two-day debate when the House returns in October?

(Mr Robertson)   That article is one brief contribution to the debate and was largely designed to answer some articles which had been appearing in that newspaper. Ms Polly Toynbee, a party colleague of yours who I think departed from the Labour Party apparently over our defence policy of the 1980s, now seems to think our old policy of the 1980s, which we have rejected, was actually something which should be embraced now.

130. If it is any comfort, I do not think she is any longer a party colleague of mine.

(Mr Robertson)   She is a very distinguished and very able journalist, and indeed a friend, so I argue on the issues rather than on the personalities of it. It was a small contribution but I am here today as Secretary of State before Parliament's own Defence Committee to establish a number of key priorities we have laid out as part of a continuing process that will take place.

131. One final question which really arises out of something Mr Blunt said. With a few alterations Mr Portillo or Mr Rifkind could have written a similar article, Mr Robertson. That is the problem for us who are anxious to get inside the thinking of the Government. What is here is entirely laudable, I do not disagree with a single word of it, but –

(Mr Robertson)   In other words, not just Mr Portillo and Mr Rifkind but also Mr Campbell, so maybe we are actually establishing a consensus. Maybe the area in which it will be more difficult to establish a consensus is when we move forward to the next stage. But Parliament has not has an opportunity of actually entering into the debate as it stands now.

132. I am not so self-confident as to want to rank myself with Mr Rifkind and Mr Portillo, but when we have the debate for two days in October we will not actually have in our discussion of the defence issues (because after all it is a two-day defence debate) the foreign policy conclusions which the Government has reached by that stage.

Do you not accept that that will mean the debate will be of a rather different character than it would have been if the Government had been able to say, 'These are the foreign policy conclusions which we have reached, now let's discuss the defence resources which are necessary to meet them'?

(Mr Robertson)   It might be reasonable to expect. If I could just say to Mr Campbell, that when we come to that debate there would be an opening speech made by the Secretary of State for Defence outlining even more of the work which will have been on-going since this point in time. I am here merely to give you some preliminary conclusions we arrived at so far. I think if we had published some document after three months and said, 'Here is our preliminary view', quite frankly, a lot of people around the table would have said, 'You achieved that remarkably quickly to go into such specific detail.' By the time the debate comes, we will be in a better position to give some more views, both about stage one and the preliminary thinking about stage two, so Parliament can then engage in that. I do not think you or anybody else is going to find it difficult to slot into a debate where they have heard from the Secretary of State at the beginning and any other contributions which may be made between now and then.

Mr Blunt

133.   There is a more important part to this surely. You will know, this is the framework, I think you told me about, the Director of Army Plans, Director of Naval Plans and the rest of it are having to work towards to generate the force structure in part two of this process. If I was the Director of Army Plans and was given this as my framework I would turn round and say: 'Well that is very interesting, this is the force structure, this is what it is, it is as it is today. In a sense there are no changes required.'

(Mr Hatfield)   I can assure you the Director of Army Plans, if he does that, will have his work rejected because I do not think you can draw that conclusion. There is a lot of continuity, the Secretary of State talked about continuity of policy, also there is continuity of British interests, of course, over a long period. So there is not surprisingly quite a lot of continuity at the moment but when you think ahead to whether you want exactly today's balance of forces and capabilities in 20 years time, even if you assume they are still pursuing the

same interests to a considerable degree, shall we say, that will not necessarily come up with the same answers. That is quite apart from, as you pointed out, looking for money from efficiency and from procurement which might help to deal with commitments. We need to look at the balance of our capabilities and within the broad themes that the Secretary of State has outlined, there are a lot of difficult issues for the Ministry of Defence to discuss. I do not think we have laid down a detailed framework yet, what we have laid down is a set of objectives which are meant to be guidance over a long period about what you are trying to achieve. What you need to do over that long period to achieve those objectives is rather more difficult, not least because things may change over time and that is the debate we are moving into now.

Mr Campbell

134. Mr Hatfield, with great respect to the Secretary of State, this is motherhood and apple pie. Indeed if you had come – with great respect to the Secretary of State – under the last administration and if the Secretary of State had then produced an article of roughly similar terms you would have made exactly the same kind of justification. What the Committee is anxious to do and what I think the defence community is desperate to do is to get some notion of what conclusions the Government is going to base its decisions on, hard decisions, as the Secretary of State rightly says, about the balance of forces, about the nature of procurement, about the nature of the deterrent. Do you not accept that we are not going to be able to take part sensibly in that second part of the discussion unless we have a clear indication of the conclusions, which have come about as a result of the opening part of the argument? If that is a case for extending the review for another two or three months, certainly I do not object to that, bringing it within a six months' framework is neither here nor there, getting it right, as the Secretary of State said, is the issue. If it takes a little longer why do we not do it that way?

(Mr Hatfield)   I think the Secretary of State has given you quite a lot of the answers but I think if you look closely at what he has said this morning, if you look at what he will say no doubt when we elaborate on it at the beginning of the defence debate, you will find there is quite a lot of conclusions about Government policy objectives in there. The Government has already separately, and the Foreign Secretary has published his mission statement for the Foreign

Office which gives you quite a few statements about the Government's foreign policy objectives, clearly we have taken those in as well although that does not start in the Review. Also we will provide a summary of what happened in the various seminars, the transcripts are available but we will provide it in a rather more convenient form. A lot of debate took place in there and there was quite a lot of contributions both from officials and indeed from the two Secretaries of State about their views.

135. Very valuable, I took part in one, I thought it was an excellent exercise and the Government is to be commended upon it. The difference between this two day defence debate and previous two day defence debates, Secretary of State, in October is we have always had a White Paper in front of us which has formed the focus of attention of the debate. We are not going to have something of that nature.

(Mr Robertson) You want something that is different, that is different! In the past you have had a crystallisation of a fixed Government position in front of Parliament and Parliament gets a sort desultory opportunity in two days of debating to wander round the territory the Government has already fixed upon. Now what we are saying in this Strategic Defence Review is exactly as we promised it. What needs to be asked and what needs to happen is a debate taking place in the country as a whole on some of these fundamentals. You may care to describe it as apple pie and motherhood as if they were components that did not matter.

136. I am sorry, I am trying to reinforce the point that we have seen it before.

(Mr Robertson) One very brief article that I have managed to get printed in the last few weeks as distinct from coming along with measured comments to this Committee, and indeed answering questions in detail on that policy framework. If we had taken the attitude and said: 'We are in power. We have a fixed idea about where we are going to go. We will write it up in the first three months. We will then bounce it into Parliament and say: "Well there you are then, now just tell us how we can configure our forces and we will probably tell you what to do there"', people would say: 'This is a con'.

137. I think you are misrepresenting my approach Secretary of State.

(Mr Robertson)   I am saying to you that this is a very different to the way defence is handled. It is a Strategic Defence Review designed to work on the basis of two great Departments of State working together and listening to the people as well. That is different I can tell you from anything I have seen in 19 years in Parliament and I think it is critically different from what people in the country expect. It used to be designed behind closed doors, stuff leaking out, rivalries between the Services, the people excluded until the last possible moment and fixed decisions then implemented. Frankly that is what has happened over the last seventeen years or so. We are doing things differently this time and giving Parliament, Members of this Select Committee and the wider public an opportunity of feeding into the process from beginning to end. I think that is commendable rather than something basically to be attacked because we are not producing firm conclusions before we have listened to the views.

Mr Campbell: I think we have exhausted that point

Chairman: Before Mr Campbell takes himself out of the Cabinet Committee to which his party has been mysteriously included.

Mr Campbell: For constitutional purposes only, robust Opposition remains our watch word.

Chairman: That is a change one has to absorb Secretary of State. I would like to ask Mr Julian Brazier to come in and then I want to push the agenda on a little more quickly.

Mr Brazier

138. Secretary of State, as you are obviously unhappy about giving us any detail on the policy base line, I wonder if you could help us on one general point on our relationship with the Foreign Office. Is this Review process being led by commitments or by capabilities? To put that just a little more precisely, is it being led by considerations of what we have to do and we can reasonably expect to have to do on the one hand or is it being led on the other by a requirement to keep certain capabilities in being because it is an uncertain world?

(Mr Robertson)   I am not entirely sure there is a distinction between the two, maybe that illustrates the danger of trying to split stage one from stage two. It is an assessment by the two departments involving the wider community in establishing what it is the country wants to do. There are some fundamental questions that have to be asked here, some of which have gone by default. Do we simply want a gendarmerie? Would the British people be happy to be what Canada is, what Sweden is at the present moment? If we chose that route would we be any good at doing it or are we in the world to play a role as a Permanent Member of the Security Council, member of the Commonwealth, part of NATO, part of the other organisations in Europe and willing to make a serious contribution to that? Are we as we promised in the election, a country wanting to be a force for good in the world and in the broader context? Those are the basic issues. They might be described by some as motherhood and apple pie. Much better than weapon systems but actually there are countries who at the present moment are savagely cutting back on their domestic defence budgets because they have opted out of any outreach role and are simply going back to territorial defence. There is only one essential superpower now left in the world and it has agonised in its Quadrennial Review about what sort of role it is going to play in the world. A lot of base closures proposed by Secretary Cohen in the Quadrennial Defence Review have been rejected by the Congress already and yet these base closures were designed to free up resources for future investment and capabilities that might be needed to deal with information warfare or some other new developments that will come. There are big choices that have to be made even in terms of initial policy but it is the policy that will actually determine what the capabilities are going to be.

139.   Can I put one more question, to be slightly more specific then, do you regard, for example, calculations whether inherited or recalculated by yourselves on issues like warning and preparation times, as forming a key part of your study, bearing in mind how often we got them wrong in the last 50 years alone?

(Mr Robertson)   Yes but we have changed them as well, sometimes wrongly but often rightly. We get it more right than most other people do in terms of readiness and timing. That is clearly part and parcel of any review, whether it is published, whether it is open, whether it is closed, it is part of normal defence planning that goes on all the time, and will be a normal part of the way that we will look at how we can deliver capabilities to our partners.

Chairman: Can we move on to a few questions on the Review procedure, John McWilliam.

Mr McWilliam

140. Secretary of State, as you know I am an old engineer and I quite like
to know how things work. What is the procedure for the review?
How often does the review team report to ministers? Which Cabinet
Ministers are involved? Are the Chiefs of Staff involved yet?

(Mr Robertson)   I will get you an answer from the official side and then give
you–

141. – the truth!

(Mr Hatfield)   It is always difficult to agree with your Secretary of State when
you are asked to speak first.

(Mr Robertson)   We do it differently.

142. I am seeking fact not opinion.

(Mr Hatfield)   I think the first thing to make clear is unlike in the case of the
Defence Cost Study, which was a different sort of review, there is not a single
review team. There are of course people within the existing structure who have
particular roles in relation to the Review and it is involving very large parts
of the Department. The answer to your other questions: clearly the Cabinet
Ministers most directly concerned are the Foreign Secretary and the Defence
Secretary and above all in the initial policy work. The balance shifts more
towards the defence end of that spectrum when we move into the detailed work
and it will be brought back to the Cabinet Overseas and Defence Committee in
the usual manner. The Chiefs of Staff are already involved in several ways,
both because they are members of the Defence Council with Ministers and of
the Financial Planning and Management Group at the top of the Department.
The Assistant Chiefs are part of the week to week steering group, if you like,
inside the Ministry of Defence which is guiding the work. Clearly their staff
and the Central Staffs who are leading the exercise are doing the day to day
work on the process. There is no specific report back every day or every week,
it is linked to pieces of work and in addition to formal bits of paper going out,
there are fairly frequent conversations. The Secretary of State fairly often asks
me how we are getting on with the work

(Mr Robertson) Can I just add to that. Because we wanted to do it differently we organised the two seminars, open public seminars which were open to the press though not many came along. They were well advertised and we hoped for wider participation. Indeed they were reported and the transcripts are going to be available. I do not think before there has been an exercise like that where you had two Secretaries of State who were there for virtually the whole of the seminars to listen to the debate that took place; three permanent secretaries at the one Mr Campbell attended in the Foreign Office; the Chief of the Defence Staff, the Vice Chief of Defence Staff and senior officials in both the Foreign Office and the Ministry of Defence. Now that was a signal of our intent to make sure we heard the views that were being expressed. Mr Campbell will vouch for the fact, I am sure, that they (*sic*) was a wide range of expert views, from single interest pressure groups to people who were distinguished in the academic community. They formed a very useful base for the thinking that took place. The politicians involved in both the Foreign Office and the Ministry of Defence are keeping a very firm handle on this and making sure all the time we are trying to generate interest outside the Ministry, outside Whitehall, to make sure that the maximum number of people become involved.

143. Given the joint report of the last committee, joint report with the Select Committee on Trade and Industry, can I press you on what is the involvement of Trade and Industry, Employment and Treasury?

(Mr Robertson) It was an interesting report, one of the few reports jointly done by Select Committees. At the moment we are involving the Foreign Office and the Ministry of Defence in our process but this is a collective Government, like all Cabinet Governments, so there will be an input from other Departments as well. The Department for International Development has got a view to express clearly about the foreign policy objectives of the Government and we talk routinely with Ministers in the Department of Trade and Industry and in the Treasury. You would expect that Treasury Ministers would keep a very close view on what is going on in discussions, and they do!

Chairman

144. Do not let them in the room.

(Mr Hatfield)   Perhaps I could add to that. At official level, we have allowed the Treasury in the room. Indeed there are arrangements for the Treasury to take an interest in all our working groups on the detailed second phase of this work, precisely because we would like to educate them into why we come whatever conclusions we come to so we have a better debate at the end. We have made specific arrangements also to involve Trade and Industry in the work on industrial aspects of the next phase and we kept them involved with the outcome in the same way as we have told you of the general outcome of our work so far. We are trying to make sure that we keep all the interests inside Government involved in the review in the appropriate way.

145.   Can I wish you well in that very ambitious project because nobody has managed to educate the Treasury since the Treasury Act 1922 but never mind.

(Mr Robertson)   Let me say to Mr McWilliam on that point, of course the Treasury have got an interest in the defence budget. It would be a very strange Treasury if it did not. And it is interested in making sure there is value for what is spent of the public money in defence; but not half as much as I have. Frankly I believe that it is our job to maximise the value we get from our defence assets. It is in the interests of our troops that we liberate money from areas of waste and duplication and to put it into the front line. I intend to be as rigorous if not more rigorous on behalf of the taxpayers, than the Treasury will be because I believe that getting value for every pound of money spent in defence is an obligation that I have on behalf of the people that elected us to power.

146.   When will the panel of academic advisers be appointed? Will their identity be made public? How large a panel do you envisage? Are any public opinion surveys being conducted in response to the review process?

(Mr Robertson)   I think September is the answer to the first question. Yes, we will publish the names is the answer to the second one. There are public opinion surveys available to us and if the panel thinks that will be a useful addition to the work we are doing then it would be something we would consider.

Ms Taylor: Secretary of State, I would like to take us back a step or two and look at some of the detail of what we could well be handling here. We are into a very valuable use of words 'coherent, strategic', you added additional words this morning 'robust, adaptable, readiness (sic) in the Armed Forces, sustainability', these are really important words and I think the Armed Forces will want to hear them. My concerns quite clearly are the concerns of many in the Armed Forces, our serving troops. Since 1979 to the present day we have lost something like a third of that fighting force, that service manpower, and my questions quite clearly therefore direct me to ask you who have we been losing? I want to know who has left the forces during this time? It is my subjective belief that we have a group that is leaving the armed forces. I feel that is possibly the least appropriate. I am asking you that question: who has been leaving, who has left the forces? Also I want to ask you, Secretary of State, will the Defence Review include a study of the size of the army? Is someone going to start attempting to establish the statement which defines appropriate size, a valued size? Are we going to end up with a size that is barely possible because of the amount of money we are prepared to commit? That level of detail if you would not mind, I see as very important.

Chairman: I think what Ms Taylor meant to say was not who left the armed forces, i.e. who has departed the armed forces, it might be quicker to say who remains in the armed forces.

Ms Taylor

147.   Absolutely.

(Mr Robertson)   The answer to that is a group of highly motivated, highly dedicated very professional people operating in many circumstances in very difficult time with reduced periods between tours. I just want to put it on record, I have been the Secretary of State now for three months, I have been to Northern Ireland, I have been to Bosnia, I have been on a Trident submarine, I have been on a fast jet out of Leuchars in Mr Campbell's constituency, I have been around a large number of establishments so far. What is so striking to me as well as to anybody else who meets our Forces is the sheer commitment that remains and the professionalism that has survived all the cuts, all of the bashing, all of the overstretch that remains. You only have to see the people working in Northern Ireland and Bosnia, for example, in Northern Ireland we have some 17,000 troops, in Bosnia – we have 5,300 troops, major commitments by the armed forces of this country to see just what is going on, commitment of very young soldiers in trying and dangerous circumstances in Northern Ireland, large numbers of people in the former Yugoslavia, in Bosnia. We are not just involved in the military operation, we are actually committed personally to

the rebuilding of a country that has been ravaged by war. I saw the soldiers of the Royal Scots Dragoon Guards with their tanks in Boraci in Bosnia who had rebuilt the school; who had themselves rebuilt the health centre, who were that week about to finish the bakery: the pivotal elements in that small town that had been invaded by the Croats, abandoned and rubbished by the Croats and now taken over by the Bosnian Serbs. But their commitment was not just simply as ordinary soldiers or as military individuals, it was as people who were there as part of a committed force, building peace, doing good, a force for good in the world. They survived all of that. I should underline that as somebody who is hugely proud of the people I serve as Secretary of State. Clearly there have been capabilities that have been lost during that period, some of which should go anyway because we had a huge commitment to the central front, to the Cold War, and to an external threat or to an external threat that has now largely disappeared. The question that now has to be answered is how we make sure the forces we have in the Army, Navy and the Air Force get the resources, the capability and the equipment to allow them to make sure that professionalism and dedication continues.

148.   Can I just ask a supplementary. I think this is a very difficult supplementary but I think we need to know: are we ending up with an armed forces which is top heavy?

(*Mr Robertson*)   No, I do not believe we are. I think we have problems with recruitment at the lower levels which are being addressed. There are some people who describe it as a crisis, there are others who say it is a temporary blip and that it will sort itself out by the year 2002. It is serious that a lot of our young people are not choosing to go into the Army, Navy and Air Force. I think as politicians we have a responsibility in that regard, we must address the problems of morale which are driving people out of the Armed Forces, and we have to do something about making sure that more young people see the Armed Forces of this country as a solid, good, stable and very rewarding career. That is what my ministers are doing at the present moment.

149.   One final question: it is clear we will have a Strategic Defence Review which will report early in the new year. We will see a review of the size of the army and the personnel and the types of people being a continuing feature of the MoD?

(*Mr Hatfield*)   The answer is yes. We are moving towards a system which has a whole series of detailed planning assumptions about what one might expect to happen over the next five years. What the Strategic Defence Review will do is provide a firm base line and then we will come back every year and see whether any of those assumptions look as if they need changing in the light of what has happened in that year. Yes, the answer is we will keep it under review, even after we have come to whatever conclusion we come to under the Strategic Defence Review.

**

Note: The section of the Minutes from 150 to 162 addressed detailed personnel questions, particularly the role of women in the Armed Forces. A brief reference was also made to the Reserve Forces. Since these discussions were concerned with the content of defence policy, rather than the process, they are omitted here. These paragraphs are available on the website http://parliament.the-stationery-office.co.uk/pa/cm199798/cmselect/cmdfence/

**

Mr Blunt

163. You were talking about the structure that is being reviewed and there are various elements obviously like Eurofighter and various procurement projects. Can you confirm the regimental system is not subject to a review, how the Army organises itself at a regimental level?

(Mr Robertson)   We have to look at all aspects of how the forces are there. I am not saying that is part of the review or that it is open to question. We have to see how we can best organise the Army, the Navy and the Air Force.

164. For instance, Mr Hatfield was saying the regimental system is being reviewed.

(Mr Hatfield)   I would not have said that, no. I would have answered the question in the way you ended it by saying we are looking at the best way of organising the Armed Forces including the Army, for future requirements. I do not draw the conclusion from that that there is a large question mark over the whole of the regimental system but I do not equally draw the conclusion there will be no changes in the way the Army organises itself. We will tell you when they have done their detailed work and no doubt hear your views as well.

Mr Campbell

165. You are not ruling out the review of the regimental system if those answers are to be understood

(Mr Robertson)   No, of course we cannot. But to say we are not ruling it out does not mean to say that suddenly it is part of an automatic change. We have said what the pillars are in our structure and the rest of it has got to be examined obviously.

Chairman: Do not touch the Staffordshire regiment otherwise you will need a new PPS!

Ms Taylor

166. A short question, Secretary of State. I was reading the House of Commons' Defence Report. This was 1996–97, and it was the final paragraph that was a bit worrying I think, putting it mildly. It said: 'We insisted that the defence spending plans set out in the 1996 Budget must be at least maintained in real terms in future years' and it adds a final kick to that statement: 'Any further reduction would jeopardise the defence of the realm.' That was the previous report, I suppose – I do not suppose, I want to ask you – are you concerned that your defence budget, our defence budget, is constrained by a precedent, by the way in which we are always wanting to spend effectively and getting as much out of our money as possible? That effectively means we spend in and around 2.5 per cent of our GDP. It is very tight. It is often very clearly seen by many of us as a straightjacket. Are you content with that situation?

(Mr Robertson)   That was a view expressed by the outgoing Defence Committee and it was after a long study of what happened in the last seventeen years.

167. Right

(Mr Robertson)   Indeed, the commitment that was given in the election by the Prime Minister to maintain the targets established by the last Government for the next two years was in many ways based on the sorts of conclusions that were being arrived at in that Report and views of other departments. More

than most the new Members who have come into this House know the gravity of the financial situation that faces the Government and the financial problems we have inherited and, therefore, the difficulties with all of the budgets has stayed. As I say, the Treasury will have its eye, as every Treasury throughout history has had its eye, on the defence budget of the country. But so do I. I will be tougher and harder on how we use our defence budget than any Treasury official or any Treasury Minister will be because we have got to make sure that it is working properly and effectively for the defence of the nation.

Chairman: I would like to move on to the question of co-operation with allies.

Mr McWilliam

    168. Have our allies been consulted about the review? What was the reaction? Will the outcome of the review be discussed with them before it is published?

(Mr Robertson) The answer to the first question, have they been consulted, is yes; they were written to. All of our key allies were written to by me on the day we made the announcement fleshing out the Defence Review. They would obviously have known in the Election manifesto what it was we were standing on but I wrote to them all giving them the details of what we were doing, the timescale, and what was involved. I have had the opportunity at both the WEU Ministerial meeting and the North Atlantic Council Meeting of defence ministers and also the NATO Summit to have further discussions with other defence ministers and to keep them briefed and aware of what it is we are conducting in this country. I think there is widespread approval for the idea of Britain looking at what needs to be done and what it can do. Some other countries are engaged in similar processes. There is obviously a cross-fertilisation of ideas between us as we go round. Clearly Defense Secretary Cohen of the United States is engaged at the present moment in selling his Quadrennial Defence Review and there is a lot of notes that can be taken on both sides about that. The answer to your final question is, yes. Of course we will inform them when we have concluded our work, and consult them about the outcome.

    169. Can you flesh out a little on your reference to the lessons being learned from the reviews that have recently taken place in other countries?

(Mr Robertson) There have been defence studies done by Australia and Canada, for instance, which one can look at. They have perhaps come to different conclusions from us in some cases but at the same time I think the Australian example would be that they very much decided that they were going to look afresh at their overseas' commitments. When I met the Australian Prime Minister, Mr John Howard, a few weeks ago, in this country – when he was buying Hawk trainers for the Australian Air Force – he took the opportunity at British Aerospace's Warton works to have a look at the Eurofighter which just happened to be parked beside the Hawks that he was buying.

Mr Campbell

170. You have just produced a very broad smile at the back of the room!

(Mr Robertson)   You have to do quite a lot as Defence Secretary but trying to sell a Eurofighter to the Australian Prime Minister at the top of a very high and precariously balanced ladder was something new in my experience. I hope that he feels buying a brand new aeroplane from me was a good bargain! Certainly I think the experience they were looking at was the fact that we have a collaborative project which has been carefully thought through and which will give a multi-role capability to this country, to Italy, Spain and Germany, and perhaps they might reap the rewards of the investment we have made.

Mr McWilliam

171. Is the UK sharing particularly with the United States and France any information or assumptions about common security risks?

(Mr Robertson)   Yes. I think we do that on a regular basis. We have, of course, a very close relationship with the United States. Secretary Cohen was appointed not long before me and we have formed a very good personal relationship as well as the one that exists between the Defence Secretaries of America and Britain. The French Government changed recently and Mr Alain Richard, who is the new French Defence Minister, was over having inner *(sic)* with me and my officials two weeks ago at Admiralty House. I think we have got a very good basis for developing and deepening bilateral relationships with France. The German Defence Minister, Volke Rühe, is an old, long standing friend of

mine. We are again engaged here in deepening bilateral relationships. Signor Andreatta, the Defence Minister of Italy, is somebody I have got to know quite well in the last three months. I think again our bilateral relationships are going to be extremely good and we will build on them. I think that they are all the critically important relationships if we are going to make sure that in Europe those who are interested in strong defence share information about threats, the opportunities, and the risks that are going to apply.

173. So you did not do what the predecessor Committee to this Committee once did which was to take our French colleagues to lunch in Wellington barracks!

(Mr Robertson) I do not know whether Admiralty House was equally inflammatory but they did not seem to show it.

173. Is the UN being consulted about future requirements for peace support operations?

(Mr Robertson) One of my early visits was to the United States and Washington. Our Ambassador out there in New York, Sir John Weston, was very careful to take me round quite a lot of the agencies that we are actively involved in. I think that the new Government's commitment to the United Nations, which was signalled first of all by rejoining UNESCO, within a couple of weeks, and indeed signing last week the Treaty of the Law of the Sea, shows quite a considerable difference to the last Government's approach to the UN. I think that approach was welcomed and will give us additional leverage in what is a very important institution.

Chairman

174. As a founder member, and indeed instigator of NATO it is obviously very central to our planning process. I had the suspicion when the Options for Change process began that NATO seemed oblivious to what was about to happen. As they have a very sophisticated planning process and need to know if and when forces are going to be available, in numbers and of what quality, have you begun discussions with those involved in the planning and financial process? Are they going to have any input as to what they would like of the United Kingdom which has been, second to the United States, the most significant member of the alliance?

(Mr Robertson)   Let me just answer at the political level and then Mr Hatfield can answer on the official level because there is a lot going on there too. At the political level we made it an absolute imperative that right at the very beginning of this process we told our allies in NATO and in the wider world precisely what it is we are about, what would be reviewed, what would not be reviewed, and the fact that old relationships were likely to continue and were going to continue as important components of both our foreign and our defence policy. I was fortunate – I do not know whether 'fortunate' is the word – to be thrown in at the deep end to the Western European Union, then the North Atlantic Council, and then the Madrid Summit. That gave me a lot of opportunities, which I took, to explain to people what it is we are about, what is not going to change and what, like other countries, we are going to have to review and consider.

Chairman: Thank you. Let us move on to a topic that would not have been on the agenda had Labour won the election in 1983 or 1987, namely Trident. Mr Campbell will ask these, whose party has gone through a similar metamorphosis!

***

Note: Paragraphs 175 to 181 discuss details of the nuclear deterrent which are not relevant to this study of strategy process, and are omitted.

***

Ms Taylor

182.   We have had the Comprehensive Spending Review identified and we have had the comprehensive review of defence identified. One of the questions which I think it would be valuable if we could hear an answer to is does the Comprehensive Spending Review involve any additional work or areas of study for the MoD on top of the Strategic Defence Review?

(Mr Hatfield) The short answer is no because our Strategic Defence Review is comprehensive. As the Secretary of State also said, if you like, for purely defence reasons we have every incentive to try and use our resources as efficiently as possible. That does not really add another dimension although we are looking at some things that will not be included in other departments' Comprehensive

Spending Reviews. If you like, our Strategic Defence Review is our contribution to the rest of what is going on round the rest of Whitehall although there is not a separate one for the MoD.

183.   Although we have had this Government Comprehensive Spending Review and the statement is that it will continue for 12 months, will the end of that Strategic Defence Review be the end of the review process within the MoD? There is a very neat difference now in the question I am asking.

(Mr Hatfield)   I think if you are asking about Reviews with a capital 'R' the answer is yes but, of course, the pressures for efficiency never go away and reviews with a small 'r' never go away. Certainly speaking as a civil servant they have not gone away in 25 years.

(Mr Robertson)   Let us establish what the Comprehensive Spending Reviews are that Government are involved in. Again they were pre-election commitments and as a member of the Shadow Cabinet before the election, I was therefore, part of the decision-making process that we must look fundamentally at all levels of spending, all areas of spending in the country. I strongly subscribe to that. That is not the Treasury versus the rest of them, a bilateral war between the Treasury and independent departments. It is a view by Government that we have to try and establish very clearly why it is we are spending public money and how effectively it is being spent. The defence budget is not immune from that process or that philosophy, and nor would it be if I was in charge of it. I believe it is important for us to justify what it is we are doing. I do not think, frankly, that a lot of people in the country realise the breakdown of the defence budget, what we spend it on and how ruthless and rigorous a lot of our procedures are. They certainly are not properly aware how savagely the defence budget of the country has been cut, especially over the last seven years. We published the Defence Statistics 1997 yesterday, showing that our defence expenditure percentage of GNP is now at the levels last seen in the 1930s. We have got to make sure that people understand what is going on. There is no ring-fencing of the defence budget because all budgets are being looked at and should be looked at. I am interested, as the departmental Secretary of State, in making sure that we get the right kit at the right time at the right price. I am not going to buy any aeroplane or any ship or any tank or bit of equipment that is not required by the Armed Forces of this country and making sure, therefore, that people are getting full value for the defence capability they voted for.

Mr Blunt

184. Presumably the review ends with all other departments in the Public Expenditure Committee at the end of your Comprehensive Spending Review process?

(*Mr Hatfield*)   I think you are asking about the process and there is a distinction which we mentioned earlier, that our Strategic Defence Review will go to the Overseas and Defence Committee of the Cabinet. Of course, the Expenditure Committee also has an interest in it but because our Review is of the strategic nature that it is, it is going to the Overseas and Defence Committee.

185. So in a sense the conclusions will be signed off by the Overseas and Defence Committee of the Cabinet?

(*Mr Hatfield*)   I imagine that it must be signed off by the Cabinet as a whole.

186. But will they make recommendations to the Cabinet?

(*Mr Robertson*) The Cabinet runs the Government so as in all of the reviews, whether it is the Strategic Defence Review which incorporates the spending review or any other departmental reviews, the same rigour will go into (*sic*) as is going into any of these other exercises.

187. The point I am making is that the Defence Review will report to the Defence Policy Committee of the Cabinet. That will obviously have a conclusion about what level of defence expenditure there is going to be, or will there not be a conclusion on defence expenditure and, therefore, will there be a subsequent meeting of the Public Expenditure Committee which will consider all the Government programmes in the round at the end of the whole process of Government and you will have to continue to have to fight for resources, even once you have concluded this process, within the fundamental expenditure review?

(*Mr Hatfield*)   I think you are trying to draw too much from the pure process point which is that the immediate work from the Defence Review will go to the Defence Committee. Most of the Comprehensive Spending Reviews, because they are coming from a difference focus, if you like, will go to the Expenditure Committee, but all of them will be considered by the Government as a whole.

You certainly cannot draw the conclusion that defence is somehow ring-fenced because of that, it is just reflecting that the Defence Review is a rather wider process.

(*Mr Robertson*) As a former special adviser you will have noticed that the personnel on the committees is largely the same. I think in a way – this should not be taken as being rude – we are splitting hairs here. There is a very deep comprehensive review taking place of the strategic view of the Government.

188.   With respect I think this is absolutely central. The Strategic Defence Review is deriving from foreign policy about what our defence requirements are going to be and you will come to a conclusion, which you will publish in the White Paper sometime early in the New Year. That is your contribution to the fundamental expenditure going on in every single department which will come to the Public Expenditure Committee of the Cabinet and at that stage it will then be resolving the limitations that are placed upon every single department as they fight for resources. My question is are you going to get involved in that issue down the line once you have published the White Paper, once presumably you have given us some indication of what public expenditure is going to be for defence? In other words, will the Defence Committee say, as we have in a report in the *Sunday Times* of the Prime Minister saying last week of his Defence Committee, 'under no circumstances is the capability of British Armed Forces to be reduced'. If that statement is to be believed as correct, the Defence Policy Committee of the Cabinet will come to the conclusion and publish the White Paper and present it to Parliament and then in effect it will also be presented to the Public Expenditure Committee where it then deals with other competing pressures on the Exchequer.

(*Mr Hatfield*)   It might be nice for the Ministry of Defence to think that is the way it works! The Comprehensive Spending Reviews are completing in very much the same timescales we are doing. Certainly I think officials in the new Ministry of Defence have been assuming the decisions on the defence requirement will be taken in the light of the Government's wider views at the time and it will not be treated in isolation. So although two are being handled slightly differently, of course we expect the Government to take an overall view. The Prime Minister is Chairman of the Cabinet, Chairman of the Defence Committee, so –

189.   But he is not Chairman of the Public Expenditure Committee.

(Mr Hatfield)   It reports to the Cabinet.

(Mr Robertson)   I think we are splitting hairs over the process.

Chairman: We did have two further areas of questioning, one on ballistic missile defence and one on procurement. I think those will be dealt with by letter, Secretary of State. We want to set you a good example by finishing our business on time although we have slightly slipped. Thank you both very much for coming. We hope that this will be the first, not of weekly meetings but more frequent meetings with the Secretary of State than we have had in the past. Thank you very much.

Annex C:
Some Examples of Evidence Collected by the House of Commons Select Committee on Defence

Submission by Oxfam on the Strategic Defence Review

Oxfam has worked alongside British troops in a number of recent complex humanitarian emergencies including Bosnia and Rwanda and on the basis of that experience, we have developed quite firm views as to what does, and does not, constitute an appropriate role for the military in these circumstances.

The Strategic Defence Review will go back to first principles in examining whether or not Britain should spend money on having a role in these situations. Oxfam's starting point is that Britain should have a substantial role to play for the following reasons:

1.   We believe that when confronted with genocide or ethnic cleansing, Britain has a moral duty to intervene in order to protect human life.

2.   We are living in an increasingly interdependent world where the politics of isolation or partial disengagement are neither possible nor desirable. In the short term, failure to invest in preventive deployments can lead to spiralling costs for humanitarian emergencies, as the Rwanda experience demonstrated. In the long

term, building a more stable and secure world is clearly in Britain's own best interests.

3.   We believe that Britain's membership of a unique range of international institutions including the UN Security Council, the G7, the Commonwealth and the EU gives it a particular responsibility for upholding the body of international law, including the Geneva Convention. It is clear that on occasions, upholding these Conventions will require military intervention.

Having established that Britain should be willing to engage in principle, the question is what kind of intervention should it contemplate in practice? On the basis of our experience, we believe that there are a number of legitimate and useful roles which the military can play within the context of complex humanitarian emergencies including:

- surveillance and intelligence gathering which contributes to early warning of potential humanitarian emergencies, provided the information is shared and acted upon;

- preventive deployment aimed at reducing the spread of conflict, as successfully happened in Macedonia;

- protection of civilians threatened by violence, for example UNAMIRs original but woefully under-resourced deployment in Rwanda;

- protection of humanitarian relief, as in Bosnia;

- the creation and policing of safe corridors or safe havens for civilians, as in Northern Iraq;

- logistical and practical support for relief efforts, for example assistance in upgrading the Goma airstrip during the Rwanda refugee crisis;

- peacekeeping once a ceasefire has been agreed, as happened in Cambodia;

- monitoring of demobilisation and decommissioning, as in El Salvador;

- the arrest of war criminals, recently demonstrated in Bosnia.

At the same time, as an operational agency, we are keen to ensure that the lines between military intervention and humanitarian intervention do not become blurred as we believe this carries risks to both sides. As governments around the world search for a new role for their armed forces in the post Cold War era, we are concerned that some, including the Dutch and Canadians, see increased military involvement in the direct delivery of humanitarian assistance as a possible solution. We would counsel very heavily against Britain following this option in the Strategic Defence Review for the following reasons:

1. We fear that increased use of the military in delivering humanitarian assistance will increase the risks faced by aid recipients and aid agencies seeking to deliver relief. The core values of humanitarian intervention are neutrality, impartiality and independence. Military intervention, on the other hand, is by definition political and will be perceived as such by actors on the ground. Where humanitarian agencies have become too closely associated with military operations, it has aroused local hostility which endangered their efforts, as was the case in Somalia.

2. There is clear evidence that the military are substantially more expensive to deploy in relief operations than civil agents such as NGOs. During the Rwanda crisis for example, the RAF was quoting cargo rates six times higher than that of a civilian airline for the transport of NGO relief supplies.

3. The military have resources and capacity designed for military emergencies rather than humanitarian ones and have, on occasions, demonstrated their inability to deliver essential services to refugees. At the height of the Goma crisis, US forces were charged by UNHCR with the task of supplying clean water to 700,000 refugees. The water purification equipment they delivered was entirely inappropriate for the task as it was tailored to keeping small numbers of soldiers in peak condition. Oxfam and UNICEF has (sic) to step in quickly to install systems designed to treat and pump large quantities of drinking water at low cost.

4.   Military culture based on the mobilisation of disciplined soldiers is ill-suited to dealing with traumatised refugees and displaced people. The military are ill-equipped to involve beneficiaries, particularly women and children, in relief efforts yet we know from experience that the involvement of beneficiaries is critical to the success of relief operations.

In conclusion, we hope that in carrying out the next phase of the Strategic Defence Review, the Government will ensure that Britain retains sufficient military capacity to uphold its international obligations and play a full role in future complex emergencies. We would warn against blurring the lines between military and humanitarian intervention as we believe this option carries with it substantial costs to both sides, but would support greater co-ordination of humanitarian and military activities in complex emergencies in order to maximise effectiveness.

Summary of Oxfam's Views on Conflict Prevention and Post-conflict Reconstruction

INTRODUCTION

The spread of conflict and the resulting increase in poverty, distress and suffering is undoubtedly the most significant challenge which Oxfam faces in the course of its work. Responding to conflict poses serious dilemmas for all of those involved, not least around the central question as to whether intervention, be it military or humanitarian, will make a given situation better or worse.

Extensive media coverage of modern conflicts invariably leads to demands that 'something must be done' but all of those involved in responding to conflict must be realistic and humble about what they can actually achieve. The role of external actors is nearly always to support, rather than replace, the initiatives of the people of the country concerned.

While the lessons learned from the conflicts of the 1990s do not point to a single blueprint for conflict prevention, there is an emerging consensus on long term risk trends and short term triggers which can be read as early warning signs of potential conflict. These point to lessons for policy, the main one being that all projects, programmes and policies should be designed in such a way as to lessen the threat posed by these risks and triggers in conflict-vulnerable and post-conflict countries.

LONG-TERM RISK TRENDS AND SHORT TERM TRIGGERS

During 1997, a range of documents from governments, multilateral organisations, aid agencies and academics broadly demonstrated an international consensus from the study of conflicts in the 1990s.

The widely-shared consensus on the main *risk trends* could be summarised as:

- Deep ethnic or religious divisions – particularly if people see that they suffer because of their group identity, and blame another group for this.

- Intense inequality and competition over resources and the means to earn a living – particularly if both are rapidly increasing.

- No democratic rule of law or institutional framework to allow peaceful change or a regulated market economy.

- A ready supply of small arms and ammunition.

The short-term *triggers* are more diverse but could be summarised as:

- Sudden widening of inequalities between social, ethnic or territorial groups, increasing the losers' sense of injustice.

- Increasingly uncertain economic prospects, heightening people's feelings of insecurity, and leading towards the aggressive accumulation of wealth.

- Weakening capacity of the state to maintain law and order, and to mediate between the winners and losers from these changes.

- Escalation of inter-communal tensions by the actions of individual leaders and political groupings – actions including the use of media and the committing of conspicuous atrocities to incite fear and hatred.

It may well be the last of these triggers which generally turn a conflict-vulnerable country into a war zone. Though many conflicts are fought along their participants' perception of dividing ethnic or religious identities, these seldom if ever lead to armed conflict without being enflamed by the actions of extreme leaders. Conflicts do not happen if they are not in someone's interest.

LESSONS FOR INTERNATIONAL POLICY

It should follow from this that *individual projects, country and regional programmes, and broad policy* should be designed to lessen the threats posed by these risks and triggers in conflict vulnerable and post-conflict countries. All projects, programmes and policies should contribute to the five broad preconditions for peaceful societies which can also be extrapolated from the experience of armed conflicts in the 1990s:

- An economy whose benefits are distributed equitably enough to provide people with secure livelihoods and a *stake in peace.*

- A formal government which is representative, not corrupt, responsive to peaceful movements for change, and encourages a sense of social cohesion through inclusive national identity, while respecting the rights of minorities.

- Vibrant civil organisations representing all sections of society, including both those who may feel excluded and those, including women's groups, who can build bridges between communities.

- An independent and effective judiciary which can punish those guilty of human rights abuses; an impartial police force; an independent media which can impartially report on abuses.

- The control of the private use of automatic weapons.

The responsibility for developing such societies lies with the governments and peoples of the countries themselves. Yet the norm is also that local efforts are either helped or hindered by international policies.

SPECIFIC POLICY PRESCRIPTIONS

Specific policy prescriptions which flow from this include the need for:

- pro-peace aid which promotes growth with equity and includes investment in basic education, health, spreading the ownership of assets (by land reform, providing access to micro-finance, and breaking monopolies) and developing small-scale agriculture and labour-intensive industry;

- support for demobilised soldiers, including for training and assistance in finding peaceful livelihoods;

- support for civil society – in post-conflict situations, civic organisations can be at the heart of rebuilding the social capital of trust undermined by conflict;

- support for justice – a stable society requires effective civil policing and an independent judiciary, so people feel that they do not have to resort to violence to protect themselves or obtain justice;

- regional support – where regional organisations are seeking to play a constructive role in building peace, international aid should support their capacity to do so. All aid channelled to countries in regions of conflict must be sensitive to the regional dimensions of instability;

- conditions for partnership – aid resources should be allocated in such a way as to reduce, not increase, the risks of armed conflict, for example favouring governments which do not indulge in excessive military expenditure;

- reducing debt – swifter and more effective action is required to reduce debt, particularly for countries such as Mozambique, struggling to reconstruct after years of conflict, and new mechanisms should be developed for addressing the issues of 'odius (sic) debt' such as that inherited from a defeated dictator, as in the Democratic Republic of Congo;

- reforming trade – an international trading regime more sensitive to the risks of war could offer the least developed countries – often those most at risk – various trading preferences including zero tariffs and more flexible rules of origin;

- support for the UN – to develop more timely recommendations for both the UN secretariat and the Security Council, Oxfam endorses calls for a UN Centre for Conflict Prevention, and for a UN rapid reaction force to protect civilians at the onset of conflicts before a peace-keeping operation for the crisis can be mobilised;

- swift and effective humanitarian action, which seeks to uphold rights to protection as well as rights to relief, and forms one part of an integrated international response;

- curbing the arms trade, by introducing a restrictive EU Code of Conduct which covers small arms and prevents the sale of arms and military equipment to countries where they might be used to abuse human rights;

- curbing the illicit trafficking of arms by making it an absolute condition of membership of the EU for countries in central Europe to demonstrate their determination to stamping out this illegal trade.

CONCLUSION

The causes of conflict are complex and multi-faceted so any attempt to design policies aimed at conflict prevention must be based on a coherent and integrated approach. One concept which is gaining ground amongst practitioners at the moment is the concept of 'conflict impact assessments' which would attempt to judge all international policies against their ability to reduce, rather than exacerbate, the risks of conflict. In its recent submission to the International Development Select Committee, Oxfam recommended that as a first step, DFID should develop a methodology for undertaking conflict impact assessments of its own programmes and projects and report its findings in its Annual Report.

Subsequently, we have suggested that DFID should encourage other Government Departments, including DTI, MoD, MAFF and FCO to undertake conflict impact assessments on appropriate areas of their own work, and ensure that the analysis of one department can be used to help another evaluate the impact of its decisions. Similarly, we have argued that conflict impact assessments should be applied to the work of multilateral institutions, non-governmental organisations and private sector ventures in conflict-prone countries. We hope that the Committee will consider this idea in drafting its own Report.

Memorandum Submitted by Professor Trevor Taylor

Royal Military College, Shrivenham
(6th May 1998)

Introduction

The preparation of the Strategic Defence Review has been extremely wide-ranging and thorough, touching all parts of the MoD. The preparation has also been time- consuming and may not be completed within a fifteen month period. Somewhat contentiously the review has been presented as 'foreign policy-led'. However the given elements of the review, such as the continued commitment to Eurofighter and Trident, have included an assumption that no additional money will be available for defence. This short paper focuses on two specific resource issues – the overall level of defence spending, where a specific recommendation is offered, and the proposed procurement reforms, where questions rather than answers are easier to identify.

The Defence Share of GDP

Arguably the review should develop a more explicit and specific resource dimension. The recommendation here is that such a dimension should include the promotion of a national consensus that the country will devote a minimum share of its GDP to the armed forces at around the current level of 2.7 per cent. This share could clearly be amended in the event of a significant change in the country's overall security situation.

The case for this position included several arguments:

a) At current costs, such a level of spending means the UK can support
flexible armed forces that can assist with the promotion of security
within the United Kingdom and make an appropriate military
contribution to the promotion of the global order. If properly
planned, such forces would also include a base structure which
could be expanded if a significant, direct conventional (*sic*) arose to
the UK or its allies.

b) The UK can afford this level of defence spending. The overall health
of the UK economy does not seem to be damaged by current levels
of defence expenditure.

c) There is a demand from the UN, NATO and indeed British public
opinion for the varied services which UK armed forces can provide.
Indeed British troops in recent years have had so little time with
their families that recruitment and retention are problematic.
Looking forward, the American defence expert William T. Johnson
has observed that 'it would be highly imprudent to assume that
global harmony will emerge by 2015' and, regarding US forces,
'the current scope and pace of operations… can be expected to
continue or increase for the foreseeable future'. These judgements
are extremely pertinent for the UK. While there are many problems
which armed forces alone cannot solve, the evidence of the last
decade is that the military can undertake a range of tasks which
moderate and even prevent many conflicts.

d) Compared with our European allies, the appropriate assessment
is not that the UK currently overspends on its military sector. A
more prudent and reasonable view is that most of them spend
too little. The current limited ability of European states to deploy
forces on international order missions is dangerous whether one
holds to a strong Atlanticist or a Eurocentric approach to security.
Europeans are increasingly vulnerable to a charge from the US
that they are not doing enough for global order. This could reduce
US readiness to support European security. 'Eurocentrics' should
also be concerned since Europeans are also unable to protect their
interests by deploying significant forces. They have to rely on
American support. A UK commitment to spend significantly but
not massively on defence should consequently be used to press
European partners to make a similar commitment.

e)   If the defence budget does not increase alongside GDP, the
        pressures for another major defence review will quickly build
        up as equipment unit costs continue to rise. Even if the 'smart
        procurement' and procurement organisation changes envisaged as
        part of the SDR are effective, they will take some years to have an
        impact. The tendency to increased unit costs is very deep-rooted
        and, while it may be moderated by new practices, it will not be
        reversed. A (presumed) UK wish to maintain forces which are
        compatible with those of the US will mean a UK requirement for
        technologically-advanced equipment. Even though more civil-
        based technology may be used in defence, defence equipment is
        often extremely complex, requiring extensive and growing systems
        integration efforts. Unlike most civilian goods, defence equipment
        has to be designed with the consideration that an adversary will
        seek actively to negate the equipment's effectiveness. This naturally
        increases cost.

f)   Even an assured share of GDP for defence would not induce
        complacency in the MoD, since the historic tendency of defence
        equipment unit costs is to rise by between 6 and 10 per cent a year.
        Even if this range is reduced through procurement improvements
        to between 4 and 6 per cent a year, which would be a great
        achievement for 'smart procurement', costs would still tend to rise
        faster than the growth in national income. The defence sector would
        therefore remain under constant pressure to be well-managed, and
        to generate continuous improvements in performance.

Committing a fairly constant share of GDP in the military instrument
would not be a novel phenomenon within NATO. Between 1978 and 1984 share
of GDP allocated to defence varied by only 0.2 per cent a year in France (3.9 to
4.1 per cent) and Germany (3.2 per cent to 3.4 per cent). A national consensus
on the share of GDP which should be allocated to defence would be a valuable
aid to effective defence planning in the UK.

Elsewhere on the defence resource and management dimension, it is
significant that the Labour Government has not reversed any of the 'New Public
Management' initiatives of the preceding regime. The Defence Cost Study/New
Management Strategy implementation is proceeding. Resource Accounting and
Budgeting is also being implemented, The Government has, however, signalled
that it wishes to introduce a different emphasis in procurement through its

'Smart Procurement' initiative and the ongoing Acquisition Organisation Review.

'Smart Procurement Issues'

The ideas involved, which to a certain extent are available in the public sector, will present a number of challenges if and when they are implemented. Will a 'system of systems' approach facilitate the faster introduction into service of new systems? How will the government decide if it wishes to use competition or a partnership with a preferred supplier for a particular acquisition or phase of an acquisition? How will smart procurement work in the context of collaborative projects? Their importance is increasing but often with countries where the UK would prefer to see a less rather than more intimate relationship between government and industry. How can the culture of government, and in particular the Procurement Executive, be changed away from a rather adversarial approach to industry to one which embraces 'partnership'? Will the UK Government feel comfortable working in a partnership relationship with defence businesses whose national character has been diluted with the European industrial restructuring which the government also favours? Given that Integrated Project teams will still be committees, how will identifiable personal responsibility for projects be increased, i.e., what will be the powers and roles of the IPT chairs? To what extent will industry be given more freedom to meet requirements without monitoring and reviews by Procurement Executive staff in order to speed up development? How will incremental acquisition work in practice in terms of equipments meeting several specified performance criteria at different points in time?

Smart procurement should represent a valuable change to government practice in an era when the limitations of competition are increasingly apparent, but it obviously will be complex to implement. Certainly, and finally, it will need to be integrated with arms export policy. Given that the UK government will be working with pre-determined preferred suppliers in many cases, it may well want those companies to be competing vigorously in external markets so as to discourage corporate complacency. The companies, insofar as they are given a voice on requirement specifications, will be keen that export potential as well as British forces' preferences are taken into account. That could lead to the government demanding a specified corporate contribution to the R&D and other fixed costs of a system. The regulation of UK arms exports, including the proposed European Code of Conduct, clearly should take these factors into account.

Conclusion

The SDR should prove of great benefit for UK defence policy, raising many important questions in terms of proposed force structures and procurement policy. The character of the UK defence debates over the past year or so has highlighted the value of stimulating an almost bottom-up review of UK defence activities. As the SDR moves to closer involvement of the Treasury, it is to be hoped that viable resource targets can be agreed which will permit the defence sector to evolve in a stable fashion while leaving in place incentives for greater efficiency within government and in industry.

Bibliography

Books and Journal Papers

Allison, G. (1971) *'Essence of Decision: Explaining the Cuban Missile Crisis'*, Harper Collins.

Allison, G. and Zelikow, P. (1999) *'The Essence of Decision: Explaining the Cuban Missile Crisis'*, 2nd Edition New York: Longman.

Andrews, K.R. (1971) *'The Concept of Corporate Strategy'*, Homewood, IL: Irwin.

Ansoff, I. (1965) *'Corporate Strategy'*, Harmondsworth: Penguin (1968 edition).

Archer, C., Ferris, J., Herwig, H. and Travers, T. (2003) *'World History of Warfare'*, London: Cassell.

Barney, J. (1991). 'Firm resources and sustained competitive advantage', *Journal of Management* Vol. 17, No. 1, pp. 99–120.

Baumgartner, F. and Jones, B.D. (1993) *'Agendas and instability in American politics'*, Chicago: University of Chicago Press.

Baylis, J. (1989) *'British Defence Policy: Striking the Right Balance'*, Basingstoke: The Macmillan Press.

Bower, J.L. (1970) *'Managing the Resource Allocation Process: A study of Corporate Planning and Investment'*, Boston: Harvard University.

Bungay, S. (2002) *'Alamein'*, London: Aurum Press.

Burgelman, R.A. (1983) 'A model of the interaction of strategic behaviour, corporate context and the concept of strategy', *Academy of Management Review* Vol. 8, No. 1, pp. 61–70.

Campbell, A. (1991) 'The Body Shop International – The most honest cosmetic company in the world'. in DeWit, B. and Meyer, R. (1994) *'Strategy: Process, Content, Context'*. First Edition, New York: West.

Campbell, A. and Yeung, S. (1991) 'Creating a sense of mission', *Long Range Planning* Vol. 24, No. 4 (August) pp. 10–20.

Carroll, L. (1865) *'Alice's Adventures in Wonderland'*, London: J.M. Dent (1949).

Chaffee, E.E. (1985) 'Three models of strategy', *Academy of Management Review* Vol. 10, No. 1. pp. 89–98.

Chalmers, M. (2002) 'The new activism', *New Economy*, London: ippr, pp. 206–211.

Clausewitz, K. von (1832) *'On War'*, edited and translated by Howard, M. and Paret, P. (1993) New York: Everyman's Library.

Cohen, M.D., March, J.G. and Olsen, J.P. (1972) 'A garbage can model of organizational choice', *Administrative Science Quarterly* Vol. 17, pp. 1–25.

Command 3999 (1998) *'The Strategic Defence Review'*, July. London: The Stationery Office.

Command 3999 (1998) *'Supporting Essays'*, London: The Stationery Office.

Command 8758 (1982) *'The Falklands: The Lessons'*, London: The Stationery Office (2001).

Cummings, S. (1995) 'Pericles of Athens – drawing from the essence of strategic leadership', *Business Horizons* Jan/Feb.

Danchev, A. and Todman, D. (eds) (2001) *'War Diaries 1939–45: Field Marshal Lord Alanbrooke'*, London: Weidenfeld and Nicholson.

De Wit, B. and Meyer, R. (2004) *'Strategy: Process, Content, Context'* (Third Edition) London: Thomson Learning.

Dutton, J.E. (1993) 'Interpretations on automatic: a different view of strategic issue diagnosis', *Journal of Management Studies* Vol. 30, No. 3, pp. 339–57.

Eldredge, N. and Gould, S.J. (1972) 'Punctuated equilibrium: an alternative to phyletic gradualism', in Schopf, J.M. (ed.) *Models in Palaeobiology* San Francisco: Freeman Cooper, pp. 82–115.

Friedman, J. (1987) *'Planning in the Public Domain'*, New Jersey: Princeton University Press.

Fry, G.K. (1981). *'The Administrative 'Revolution' in Whitehall'*, London: Croom Helm.

Gardner, R. (2009) 'UK defence on the edge', *Aerospace International* April pp. 28–32.

Grattan, R.F. (2002) *'The Strategy Formulation Process: A military-business comparison'*, Basingstoke: Palgrave Macmillan.

Grattan, R.F. (2009a) *'The Origins of Air War: The development of military air strategy in World War 1'*, London: I.B Tauris.

Grattan, R.F. (2009b) 'On the origins of strategy', *Strategy and Defence* Issue 1/2009 (www.defenceandstrategy.eu).

Gray, C. (1999) 'Why strategy is difficult', *Joint Force Quarterly* No. 22, pp. 6–12

Halperin, M.H. (1974) *'Bureaucratic Politics and Foreign Policy'*, Washington DCL Brookings Institute.

Hamel, G. and Prahalad C.K. (1993) 'Strategy as stretch and leverage', *Harvard Business Review* March/April pp. 75–84.

Handy, C (1990) *'Inside Organizations'*, London: BBC Books.

Hax, A. (1990) 'Redefining the Concept of Strategy', *Planning Review* May/June.

Hermann, C. F. (1963) 'Some consequences of crisis which limit the viability or organizations', *Administrative Science Quarterly* Vol. 21, pp. 41–65.

Hobbes, T. (1651) *'The Leviathan'*, Cambridge: Cambridge University Press (1994).

Howard, M. (1970) 'Lord Haldane and the Territorial Army', in *Studies in War and Peace*, London: Temple Smith.

ippr (2009) *'Shared Responsibilities: A National Security Strategy for the UK'*, The Final Report of the ippr Commission on National Security in the 21st Century.

Ismay, Lord (1960) *'The Memoirs of Lord Ismay'*, London: Heinemann.

Jackson, B. and Bramall, E. (1992) *'The Chiefs: The Story of the United Kingdom Chiefs of Staff'*, London: Brasseys.

Jarzabkowski, P. (2005) *'Strategy as Practice: An Activity-based Approach'*, London: SAGE Publications.

Johnson, A.H. (1909) revised 1955 *'The Age of the Enlightened Despot 1660–1789'*, London: Methuen.

Kanter, R.M. (1983) *'The Change Masters'*, New York: Simon and Schuster.

Kennedy, J.F. (1963) *'Preface'* to Sorensen, T. (1963) *'Decision-Making in the White House: The Olive Branch and the Arrows'*, New York: Columbia University Press (Quoted in Allison and Zelikow (1999: xv) *qv*.

Koistinen, P.A.C. (1980) *The Military-Industrial Complex: A Historical Perspective* New York: Praeger

Laffin, M. and Alys, T. (1997) 'New Labour and government in Britain: change or continuity?', *Australian Journal of Public Administration* Vol. 56, No. 4 (Dec) p. 117.

Liddell Hart, B.H. (1929) *'The Decisive Wars of History'*, London: G.Bell & Sons.

Lindblom, C.E. (1959) 'The science of muddling through', *Public Administrative Review* Vol. 19, pp. 79–88.

Lloyd George, D. (1936) *'War Memoirs'*, Two Volumes, London: Odhams Press.

Low, Sir Sidney (1904) *'The Government of England'*, London: Unwin.

McInnes, C. (1998) 'Labour's Strategic Defence Review', *International Affairs* Vol. 74, Issue. 4, pp. 823–846.

Marwick, A. (1965) *'The Deluge: British society and the First World War'*, London: The Macmillan Press.

Mason, R. and Mitroff, I. (1981) *'Challenging Strategic Planning Assumptions'*, New York: Wiley.

May, E.R. and Zelikov, P.D. (eds) (2002) '*The Kennedy Tapes*', New York: W W Norton.

Miller, D. (2003) '*Political Philosophy: A Very Short Introduction*', Oxford: Oxford University Press.

Mintzberg, H. and Walters, J.A. (1985) 'Of strategies, deliberate and emergent', *Strategic Management Journal* Vol. 6, pp. 257–72.

Mintzberg, H. (1987) 'The strategy concept: five Ps for strategy', *California Management Review* Fall, pp. 11–24.

Mintzberg, H. (1990) 'The Design School: reconsidering the basic premises of strategic management', *Journal of Strategic Management* Vol. 11 (March), pp. 171–95.

Mintzberg, H. (1991) 'The effective organisation: forces and forms', *Sloan Management Review* (Winter), pp. 54–66.

Mintzberg, H. (1994) 'Rethinking Strategic Planning Part II: New Roles for Planners', *Long Range Planning* Vol. 27, No. 3, pp. 22–28.

Mottram, R. (1991) 'Options for Change: Process and Prospects', *Journal of the Royal United Services Institute for Defence Studies*, Spring.

Ovendale, R. (1994) '*British Defence Policy Since 1945*', Manchester: Manchester University Press.

Papadakis, V., Kaloghirou, Y. and Iatrelli, M. (1999) 'Strategic decision making: from crisis to opportunity', *Business Strategy Review* Vol. 10, No. 1, pp. 29–37.

Pascale, R. and Athos A. (1982) '*The Art of Japanese Management*', London: Allen Lane.

Peters, T. and Waterman, R. (1982) '*In Search of Excellence*', New York: Harper Colins.

Pettigrew, A. (1988) '*The Management of Strategic Change*', Oxford: Basil Blackwell.

Pettigrew, A. (1992) 'The character and significance of strategy process research', *Strategic Management Journal* Vol. 13, Special Issue, Winter pp. 5–16

Ponting, C. (1986) '*Whitehall: Tragedy and Farce*', London: Sphere Books.

Portillo, M. (ed.) (1997) '*British Defence Doctrine: JWP 0-01*', London: Her Britannic Majesty's Stationery Office.

Prahalad, C.K. and Hamel, G. (1990) 'The Core Competence of the Corporation', *Harvard Business Review* May–June pp. 79–91.

Quinn, J.B. (1978) 'Strategic Change: "Logical Incrementalism"', *Sloan Management Review* Autumn. Reprinted Summer 1989 pp. 45–60.

Rawnsley, A. (2001) '*Servants of the People*'. Harmondsworth: Penguin Books.

Rittel, H.W.J. and Webber, M.M. (1973) 'Dilemmas in a general theory of planning', *Policy Sciences* 4, pp. 155–169.

Robinson, P. (2005) *'Doing Less with Less: Making Britain More Secure'*, Exeter: Imprint Academic.

Rumelt, R. (1980) 'The evaluation of business strategy', in de Wit, B. and Meyer, R. (1994) *'Strategy: Process, Content, Context'* (1ˢᵗ Edition), pp. 186–192.

Sabin, P.A.G. (1993) 'British defence choices beyond "options for change", *International Affairs* Vol. 69, No. 2, pp. 267–287.

Schoemaker, P. (1992) 'How to link vision to core capabilities', *Sloan Management Review,* Fall, pp. 67–81.

Select Committee on Defence (1998) Eighth Report – The Strategic Defence Review 10ᵗʰ September 1998, London: House of Commons.

Simon, H.A. (1976) *'Administrative Behavior'*, Third Edition, New York: The Free Press.

Stalk, G., Evans, P. and Shulman, L. (1992) 'Competing on Capabilities', *Harvrad Business Review* March/April pp. 57–69.

Testar, S. (1997) 'The Defence Review Process 1643–1939', University of Hull. Paper submitted to the Parliamentary Select Committee on Defence, used in their report but not now accessible.

Thorngate, W. (1976) '"In general" vs "It depends": some comments on the Gergen-Schlenker debate', *Personality and Social Psychology Bulletin* Vol. 2, pp. 404–410.

Tsouras, P.G. (ed.) (2005) *'Dictionary of Military Quotations'*, London: Greenhill Books.

Vagts, A. (1959) *'A History of Militarism'*, New York: The Free Press.

Wintour, P. (1998) 'Arms and the strategy men: Defence is putting on a new face', London: *The Observer* newspaper, July 5th p. 21.

Internet

Ashdown, Lord (2009) 'National Security? Include us in', *Institute for Public Policy Research* paper, 17th August 2009 www.ippr.org/articles/?id=3667

Edwards, T. (2009) 'UK Defence Policy: Implications for Equipment and Budget – "A Decision the next Prime Minister must make..."' p. 24, www.uknda. org

Hansard (1997) Debate in the House of Commons 27th October, www. publications.parliament.uk/pa/cm199798/cmhansard/vo971027/debtext

Hansard (1997 Debate in the House of Lords 6th November, www.publications. parliament.uk/pa/ld199798/ldhansard/vo971106/text/71106-03.htm

House of Commons: Sixth Special Report, www.publications.parliament.uk/
    pa/cm199798/cmselect/cmdfence/1198/11980

Lodge, G. (2006) 'The paradox of permanence and its effect on reform', Solace
    1 Jan 2006 and www.ippr.org.uk/articles/index.asp?id=1935

Select Committee on Defence Eighth Report, http://www.publications.
    parliament.uk/pa/cm199798/cmselect/cmdfence

Index

Figures are indicated by **bold** page numbers, tables by *italic* numbers.